Prince or Cha
A Story of N

Lawrence Perry

Alpha Editions

This edition published in 2024

ISBN 9789362095732

Design and Setting By

Alpha Editions
www.alphaedis.com

Email - info@alphaedis.com

As per information held with us this book is in Public Domain.
This book is a reproduction of an important historical work.
Alpha Editions uses the best technology to reproduce historical work
in the same manner it was first published to preserve its original nature.
Any marks or number seen are left intentionally to preserve.

Contents

CHAPTER I THE MIDNIGHT EXPRESS	- 1 -
CHAPTER II MISS WELLINGTON ENLARGES HER EXPERIENCE	- 6 -
CHAPTER III PRINCE VASSILI KOLTSOFF	- 15 -
CHAPTER IV THE TAME TORPEDO	- 24 -
CHAPTER V AT TRINITY	- 31 -
CHAPTER VI AN ENCOUNTER WITH A SPY	- 35 -
CHAPTER VII MISS WELLINGTON CROSSES SWORDS WITH A DIPLOMAT	- 39 -
CHAPTER VIII WHEN A PRINCE WOOS	- 45 -
CHAPTER IX ARMITAGE CHANGES HIS VOCATION	- 50 -
CHAPTER X JACK MCCALL, AT YOUR SERVICE	- 56 -
CHAPTER XI THE DYING GLADIATOR	- 65 -
CHAPTER XII MISS HATCH SHOWS SHE LOVES A LOVER	- 73 -
CHAPTER XIII ANNE EXHIBITS THE PRINCE	- 78 -
CHAPTER XIV UNDERGROUND WIRES	- 86 -
CHAPTER XV ANNE AND SARA SEEK ADVENTURE	- 93 -
CHAPTER XVI THE ADVENTURE MATERIALIZES	- 98 -
CHAPTER XVII THE NIGHT ATTACK	- 102 -
CHAPTER XVIII ANNE WELLINGTON HAS HER FIRST TEST	- 110 -
CHAPTER XIX AN ENCOUNTER IN THE DARK	- 116 -
CHAPTER XX WITH REFERENCE TO THE DOT	- 123 -
CHAPTER XXI PLAIN SAILOR TALK	- 129 -

CHAPTER XXII THE BALL BEGINS — 135 -

CHAPTER XXIII THE BALL CONTINUES — 141 -

CHAPTER XXIV THE BALL ENDS — 147 -

CHAPTER XXV THE EXPATRIATE — 154 -

CHAPTER XXVI CONCLUSION — 159 -

CHAPTER I
THE MIDNIGHT EXPRESS

John Armitage, Lieutenant U. S. N., followed the porter into the rear car of the midnight express for Boston, and after seeing his bag deposited under a lower berth, stood for a minute in frowning indecision. A half-hour must elapse before the train started. He was not a bit sleepy; he had, in fact, dozed most of the way from Washington, and the idea of threshing about in the hot berth was not agreeable. Finally, he took a short thick pipe from his pocket, and picking his way gingerly between the funereal swaying curtains and protruding shoes, he went outside to talk to the porter.

The features of this functionary relaxed, from the ineffable dignity and self-containment of a dozing saurian, into an expression of open interest as Armitage ranged alongside, with the remark that it was cooler than earlier in the evening.

"Ya'as, suh," agreed the porter, "it sut'nly am mighty cooler, jes' now, suh." He cocked his head at the young officer. "You 's in de navy, suh, ain't you, suh? I knowed," he added, as Armitage nodded a bored affirmative, "dat you was 'cause I seen de 'U. S. N.' on yo' grip. So when dat man a minute ago asked me was dere a navy gen'lman on my cyar, why I said—"

"Eh!" Armitage turned upon him so quickly that the negro recoiled. "Asked for me! Who? What did he say? When did he ask?"

"I came outen the cyar after cahying in yo' bag, Majah," replied the porter, unctuously, "and dey was a man jes' come up an' ask me what I tole you. 'Ya'as, suh,' says I, 'I jes' took in de Kunnel's bag.' So he goes in an' den out he comes again, givin' me fifty cents, an' hoofed it out through de gates, like he was in a hurry."

Armitage regarded the negro strangely.

"What did he look like?" he asked. "Quick!"

"He was a lean, lanky man wid a mustache and eye-glasses. He looked like a foreigner. He—"

But Armitage had started on a run for the iron gates. In the big waiting-room there were, perhaps, a score of persons, dozing or reading, no one of whom resembled the man described by the porter. He passed across to the telephone booths and as he did so the one for whom he was searching emerged from the telegraph office, walked rapidly to the Forty-second Street doors, and jumped into a taxi-cab waiting at the curb.

And so Armitage missed him. He walked back to the train with a peculiar smile, emotions of pleasurable excitement and a sense of something mysterious conflicting.

"Missed him," he said in answer to the porter's look of inquiry.

"Friend of yo's, suh?"

"Well," said the officer, smiling grimly, "I should have liked to shake hands with him."

His desire would have been keener could he in any way have known the nature of the message which the curious stranger had sent to a squalid little house on William Street in Newport:

A. leaves here for torpedo station on midnight train.

Though he did not know it, despatches of a similar nature had been following or preceding him these past three months, a fact certainly not uncomplimentary to an officer who had been out of the academy a scant ten years, whatever the additional aspects.

As it was, Armitage, not given to worrying, dismissed the incident for the time being and yielded full attention to the voluble porter. The young officer was from Kentucky, had been raised with negroes, and understood and liked them thoroughly.

With five minutes remaining before midnight he was about to knock the fire from his pipe when a bustle at the gate attracted his attention. A party, two women, their maids, and a footman bearing some luggage, was approaching the train. The older woman was of distinguished bearing and evidently in no amiable mood; the younger was smiling, trying to pacify her.

"Well, mother," she said, as the party stopped at Armitage's car, "the worst of the ordeal is over. It has all been so funny and quite exciting, really."

That she was an interesting girl, Armitage could see even in the ghastly effulgence of the arc lamps. Slightly above the medium height, with a straight, slim figure, she was, he judged, about twenty-two or three years old. Her light hair flowed and rippled from under a smart hat; her face, an expressive oval; her mouth not small, the lips full and red. Armitage could not tell about the eyes, but considering her hair and vivid complexion they were, he decided, probably hazel. From his purely scientific or rather artistic investigation of the girl's face, he started suddenly to find that those eyes were viewing him with an unmistakably humorous disdain. But only for a second. Then as though some mental picture had been vaguely limned in her mind, she looked at him again, quickly, this time with a curious expression, as of a person trying to remember, not quite certain whether she should bow. She did n't. Instead, she turned to her mother, who was advancing toward the porter, voicing her disapproval of her daughter's characterization of the situation.

"Funny! exciting!" she exclaimed. "You are quite impossible, Anne. Porter, is this our car?"

The negro examined the tickets and waved his hand toward the steps.

"Ya'as'm, cyar five; state room A, an' upper 'n lower ten, for dem ladies," indicating the maids. "Ya'as'm, jes' step dis way."

With a few directions to the footman, who thereupon retraced his steps to the station, the woman followed her daughter and the maids into the car. A minute or so later the train was rolling out into the yard with its blazing electric lights, and Armitage, now hopelessly wakeful, was in the smoking compartment, regarding an unlighted cigar. Here the porter found him.

"Say, Gen'ral," he said, "dem folks is of de vehy fust quality. Dey had got abo'd dey yacht dis ebenin', so dey was sayin', an' somethin' was broke in de mashinery. So dey come asho' from whar dey went on de ship at de yacht club station. Dey simply hab got ter get to Newport to-morrow, kase dey gwine receive some foreign king or other an'—"

"Sam," interrupted Armitage, "did you find out who they are?"

"Ya'as, suh. Ah sut'nly did," was the pompous reply. "Dey is de Wellingtons."

"Wellington," Armitage regarded the porter gravely. "Sam, I have been in Newport off and on for some time, but have been too busy to study the social side. Still, I happen to know you have the honor of having under your excellent care, the very elect of society."

"Well, dey only gib me fifty cents," grimaced the porter, "an' dat don' elect 'em to nothin' wid me."

Armitage laughed.

"You were lucky," he said. "You should have paid them for the honor."

The porter shook his head gloomily. "Two bits," he growled. "I don' see no sassiety partiality in dat."

"No," Armitage reached into his pocket; "Here, Sam, is fifty cents for hefting that young woman's bag." He paused and smiled. "It is the nearest I have ever come to paying the bills for such a beautiful creature. I like the experience. Now don't forget to call me at Wickford Junction, or the other people either; for when I get them aboard the *General* I am going to start a mutiny, throw the mater overboard, and go to sea. For, Sam, I rather imagine Miss Wellington glanced at me as she boarded the train."

The porter laughed, pocketing the silver piece, and left Armitage to his own devices. He sat for a long time, still holding the unlighted cigar, smiling quizzically. Some underlying, romantic emotion, which had prompted his vicarious tip to the porter, still thrilled him; and it was not until the train had flashed by Larchmont, that he went to his berth.

The full moon was swimming in the east, bathing the countryside in a light which caused trees and hills, fences and bowlders to stand out in soft distinctness. Armitage raised the window curtain and lying with face pressed almost against the pane, watched the ever-changing scenes of a veritable fairyland. He was anything but a snob. He was not lying awake because a few select representatives of the Few Hundred happened to be in his car. Not by a long shot. But that girl, he admitted, irrespective of caste, was a cause for insomnia, good and sufficient.

"Anne!" He muttered the name to himself. By George, it fitted her! He did not know they bred her sort in the Newport cottage colony. Armitage was sufficiently conceited to believe that he knew a great deal about girls. He had this one placed precisely. She was a good fellow, that he would wager, and unaffected and unspoiled, which, if he were correct in his conjectures, was a wonderful thing, he told himself, considering the environment in which she had been reared.

"I may be wrong, Anne Wellington," he said to himself, "but I 've an idea we 're going to know each other better. At any rate, we, speaking in an editorial sense, shall strive to that end."

He chose to ignore the obvious difficulties which presented themselves in this regard. Who were the Wellingtons? His great, great grandfather was signing the Declaration of Independence when the Wellingtons were shoeing horses or carrying sedan chairs in London. His father was a United States Senator, and while Ronald Wellington might own one or two such, he could not own Senator Armitage, nor could any one else.

The train flashed around the curve into Greenwich and the Sound appeared in the distance, a vast pool of shimmering silver. Armitage started.

"That torpedo of mine could start in that creek back there and flit clean into the Sound and chase a steel hull from here to Gehenna. In two weeks I 'll prove it."

How had Anne Wellington suggested his torpedo? Or was it the moonlight? Well, if he set his mind on his torpedo he would surely get no sleep. It had cost him too many wakeful hours already. He lowered the curtain and closed his eyes.

CHAPTER II
MISS WELLINGTON ENLARGES HER EXPERIENCE

Few places in the well-ordered centres of civilization are so altogether dreary as Wickford Junction, shortly before five o'clock in the morning, when the usual handful of passengers alight from the Boston express. The sun has not yet climbed to the top of the seaward hills of Rhode Island, the station and environment rest in a damp semi-gloom, everything shut in, silent—as though Nature herself had paused for a brief time before bursting into glad, effulgent day.

The station is locked; one grocery store in the distance presents a grim, boarded front to the sleeping street. No one is awake save the arriving passengers; they are but half so, hungry and in the nature of things cross. Mrs. Wellington was undisguisedly in that mood.

Armitage found some degree of sardonic pleasure in watching her as she viewed with cold disapproval the drowsy maids and her daughter, who although as immaculate and fresh and cool and altogether delightful as the morning promised to be, persisted in yawning from time to time with the utmost abandon. Armitage had never seen a woman quite like the mother. Somewhat above medium height, there was nothing in the least way matronly about her figure; it had still the beautiful supple lines of her youth, and her dark brown hair was untinged by the slightest suggestion of gray. It was the face that portrayed the inexorable progress of the years and the habits and all that in them had lain. Cold, calculating, unyielding, the metallic eyes dominated a gray lineament, seamed and creased with fine hair-like lines.

No flippant, light-headed, pleasure-seeking creature of society was Belle Wellington. Few of her sort are, public belief to the contrary notwithstanding. Her famous fight for social primacy, now lying far behind in the vague past, had been a struggle worthy of an epic, however meticulous the object of her ambition may have appeared in the eyes of many good people. At all events she had striven for a goal not easy of attainment.

Many years before, on the deck of her husband's yacht—whither, by methods she sternly had forgotten, had been lured a select few of a select circle—the fight had begun. Even now she awoke sometimes at night with a shudder, having lived again in vivid dream that August afternoon in

Newport Harbor, when she sat at her tea table facing the first ordeal. She had come through it. With what rare felicity had she scattered her conversational charms; with what skill had she played upon the pet failings and foibles of her guests; what unerring judgment had been hers, and memory of details, unfailing tact, and exquisite taste! A triumph, yes. And the first knowledge of it had come in a lingering hand clasp from the great man of them all and a soft "dear" in the farewell words of his wife. But she had fainted in her cabin after they left.

Since that day she had gone far. She was on familiar terms with an English earl and two dukes; she had entertained an emperor aboard her yacht; in New York and Newport there were but two women to dispute her claims as social dictator, and one of these, through a railroad coup of her husband's, would soon be forced to her knees.

It was all in her face. Armitage could read it there in the hard shrewd lines, the cold, heartless, vindictive lines, or the softer lines which the smiles could form when smiles were necessary, which was not so often now as in former years. And in place of the beauty now gone, she ruled by sheer power and wit, which time had turned to biting acidity,—and by the bitter diplomacy of the Medicis.

"Ugh!" Armitage drew his pipe from his pocket with humorous muttering. "A dreadnaught, all right. An out-and-out sundowner. And I beg leave to advise myself that the best thing about fair Anne is that she favors her father, or some relative considerably more saintly than My Lady of the Marble Face."

As Armitage passed the group in pacing the platform, the woman whom he had been studying raised her eyes and gazed at him with just a touch of imperiousness.

"I beg your pardon," she said, and a trace of the little formal smile appeared; "but can you tell me when we are to have a train?"

Armitage glanced at his watch.

"It is due now," he said, "I think—here it comes," he added, inclining his head towards a curve in the track around which a little locomotive was pushing two dingy cars.

Mrs. Wellington nodded her thanks and turned to her daughter, as though dismissing Armitage, who, indeed, had evinced no desire to remain, walking toward the upper end of the platform where his bag reposed upon a pile of trunks.

He did not see them again until they boarded the *General* at Wickford Landing for the trip down Narragansett Bay. They were all in the upper cabin, where Mrs. Wellington was evidently preparing to doze. Armitage walked forward and stood on the deck under the pilot house, watching the awakening of the picturesque village across the narrow harbor, until the steamboat began to back out into the bay. The sunlight was glorious, the skies blue, and the air fresh and sparkling. Armitage faced the breeze with bared head and was drawing in deep draughts of air when footsteps sounded behind him, and Anne Wellington and her maid came to the rail.

"How perfectly delightful, Emilia," she exclaimed. "Now if I could have a rusk and some coffee I should enjoy myself thoroughly. Why don't they conduct this boat like an English liner!"

Her eyes, filled with humorous light, swept past Armitage; yes, they were hazel.

"I am so hungry, Emilia!" She smiled and sniffed the air with mock ardor. "Emilia, did n't you smell that tantalizing odor of hot biscuits in the cabin? I wonder where it came from."

Armitage suddenly remembered a previous journey in this boat and he was on the point of addressing the girl when he checked himself, but only for a minute. Her mother had addressed him in her presence, had she not? Certainly that constituted, well, if not an acquaintance, at least something which involved warrant to assist her in time of stress, which he decided to be here and now.

So he turned to the girl with that boyish grin and that twinkling of his clear, gray eyes which people found so contagious in him, and addressed her in the most natural way.

"If I don't intrude egregiously—" He rounded out this beautiful word, a favorite of his father's, with a drawling, tentative inflection, which caused Anne to smile in spite of herself. Seeing which Armitage continued: "I happen to know that the steward in the galley below makes biscuits and brews coffee at this hour each morning such as are given to few mortals. If you 'll allow me the honor of playing waiter, I 'll be delighted to serve you in the cabin."

"If you'll allow me the honor of playing waiter, I'll be delighted to serve you in the cabin."

"If you'll allow me the honor of playing waiter, I'll be delighted to serve you in the cabin."

Anne Wellington heard him in wide-eyed astonishment. Then she laughed, not at all affectedly, and glanced swiftly through the cabin windows, to where her mother sat apparently in slumber.

"I thank you. It's awfully polite of you. But you needn't play waiter. Instead—would it be too much trouble for you to show us where the—the—"

"Galley," suggested Armitage.

"Where the galley is?"

Armitage hesitated.

"No," he said, "it would be a pleasure. Only, the galley, or, rather, the mess room, is rather a stuffy place. I—"

"Oh, I should n't mind that in the least. I am not unused to roughing it." She turned to her maid. "Emilia, go and tell Morgan to say to mother, if she wakes, that we are in the galley, breakfasting on plum duff."

Armitage said nothing while they waited for her return. Anne Wellington was silent, too. She simply stood waiting, tapping the toe of one of her small russet pumps on the deck and gazing out over the bay with a curious little smile rippling up from the corner of her mouth.

Armitage did not quite understand her. While she had been cordial enough, yet there was an underlying suggestion of reserve, not at all apparent and yet unmistakably felt. It was, he felt, as though in her life and training and experience, she had acquired a poise, a knowledge of at least certain parts of the world and its affairs, which gave her confidence, made her at home, and taught her how to deal with situations which other girls less broadly endowed would have found over-powering, or, at best, distinctly embarrassing.

Not that Armitage had in any way sought to embarrass Miss Wellington. He had spoken simply upon impulse, being of that nature, and he could not but admire the way in which she had diagnosed his motive, or rather lack of motive save a chivalrous desire to serve. Evidently she had long been accustomed to the homage of men, and more, she was apparently a girl who knew how to appraise it at its true value in any given case. If Armitage had but known it, this was a qualification, not without its value to the girls and elder women who occupied Anne Wellington's plane of social existence. The society calendar of scandal is mainly a list of those who have not possessed this essential.

When the maid returned, Miss Wellington smiled and nodded to Armitage, who led the way into the cabin and to the main stairway and thence down into the hold.

The steward was a bustling, voluble little man with well-rounded proportions and a walrus-like mustache. As Armitage and his two companions entered, he was engaged in removing a coffee-stained table cover—the crew had finished breakfasting—which he replaced with a spotless red-and-white checkered cloth.

"Steward," said Armitage, falling unconsciously into the crisp voice of command, "get some coffee and biscuits for this lady and her maid, please."

"Yes, sir," the steward smiled affably, "certainly, sir. They're fine this morning—the biscuits, I mean. Fine!"

"Very good," said Armitage. He pulled two chairs to the table and was leaving the room when the girl looked over her shoulder.

"Are n't you going to join us?" she asked.

"Well," said Armitage smiling, "I was going to breakfast in the galley. It is so warm by the range, you know."

"Nonsense! Don't mind us. It's rather novel breakfasting with one's maid—and a stranger."

She said this in rather an absent manner, as though the fact to which she called attention were almost too obvious for remark. Certainly it was not said in any way to impel Armitage to introduce himself, and he had no wish to take advantage of a lame opportunity.

"Yes," he said, seating himself at one end of the table; "it impresses me that way, too."

To say that the biscuits were delicious and the coffee uplifting, inspiring, would, in the mind of all who have shared the matutinal hospitality of the steward of the *General*, be an inadequate expression of gastronomic gratitude. Let it be sufficient to note that Anne Wellington beamed gratefully upon the steward, who, expanding under the genial influence, discussed his art with rare unction.

"The secret," he said, leaning confidentially over the back of Miss Wellington's chair, "is to be sparin' of the yeast; and then there is somethin' in raisin' 'em proper. Now, the last time Mrs. Jack Vanderlip was down here, she made me give her the receipt for them identical biscuits; gave me a dollar for it."

"Mrs. Jack Vanderlip!" cried Miss Wellington, "did she ever grace your table?"

"Did she ever grace this table! Well, I should say so, and the Tyler girls and Hammie Van Rensselaer and Billy Anstruther,—he comes down here often."

Miss Wellington laughed.

"I often have marvelled at Billy's peach-blow complexion," she said; "now I have the secret."

"Don't tell him I said so, Miss Wellington," said the steward.

The girl, with a biscuit poised daintily in her fingers, did not seem surprised to hear her name.

"Your acquaintance is rather exten—rather large," she said.

The steward actually blushed.

"I live in Newport, miss," he said.

"Oh!" That was all, and the curious little smile did not leave her face. But Armitage noticed that in some way the steward found no further opportunity for exercising his garrulity.

Evidently she assumed that Armitage now knew whom she was, if he had not known before the steward uttered her name, for he noticed a slight modifying of her previous attitude of thorough enjoyment. For his part, Armitage of course had no reason for altering his bearing, and that he did not was observed and appreciated by his companion. This eventually had the effect of restoring both to their former footing.

"Yes," she said finally, "it has been rather a novel experience. I am indebted to you."

"Not to me," said Armitage. Then, by way of conversation, "novel experiences, as a rule, are not so easily had."

"No, I grasp them whenever," she jerked her head toward the cabin above and smiled, "whenever I can, conveniently. My old tutor in Munich was always impressing it upon me never to neglect such opportunities."

"Opportunities? Oh, I see—slumming." Armitage glanced about the apartment and laughed.

She frowned.

"I was speaking categorically, not specifically; at least I meant to. I did not mean slumming; I detest it. '*Seine erfahrungen erweitern*'—enlarging one's experience—is the way my teacher put it. Life is so well-ordered with us. There are many well-defined things to do—any number of them. The trouble is, they are all so well defined. We glide along and take our switches, as father would say, like so many trains." She smiled. "And so I love to run off the track once in a while."

"May I have the credit of having misplaced the switch?" Armitage's eyes were twinkling as the girl arose with a nod.

In the upper cabin, Mrs. Wellington, apparently, still slept, to Armitage's great joy. Her daughter, with hardly a glance into the cabin, stepped to the rail and looked down the bay with radiant face. The promise of the early hours had been established; it was a beautiful day. It was one of these mornings typical of the hour; it looked like morning, smelt like morning, there was the distinct, clean, pure, inspiring feel of morning. The skies were an even turquoise with little filmy, fleecy shreds of clouds drifting across; the air was elixir; and the blue waters, capped here and there with white, ran joyously to meet the green sloping shores, where the haze still lingered. Ahead, an island glowed like an opal.

"Perfect, perfectly stunning!" cried the girl. Somehow Armitage felt the absence of that vague barrier which, heretofore, she had seemed almost unconsciously to interpose, as her eyes, filled with sheer vivacity, met his.

"What are those little things bobbing up and down in the water over there?" she asked.

"I believe that is the torpedo testing ground," he said.

"Torpedoes! Ugh!" She shrugged her shoulders. "Mother knew Vereshchagin, who was in the *Petrapavlovsk* when she struck the Japanese torpedo and turned upside down. Do you know anything about torpedoes?"

"Not much; a little." Armitage thrilled at the first sign she had given him that she considered or was in any way curious regarding his personality.

She looked at him.

"I am certain I have seen you before," she said. "You don't live in Newport?"

"That is not my home," said Armitage. "I come from Kentucky. I am something of a wanderer, being a sort of fighter by profession."

The girl started.

"Not a prize fighter?" She glanced quickly at the handsome, square, fighting face, the broad chest and shoulders, and flushed. "Are you really that?"

Armitage had intended to tell her he was a naval officer, but obsessed of the imp of mischief, he nodded.

"I can imagine situations wherein I might fight for a prize."

She overlooked what she regarded as the apparent modesty of his answer.

"Really!" she exclaimed. "How interesting! Now I am glad I met you. I had no idea you were that, of all things. You seemed—" She checked herself. "But tell me, how did you begin? Tommy Dallas is keen on your sort. Did he ever—ever back you, I believe he calls it—in a fight?"

The new trend speedily had become distasteful to Armitage, who inwardly was floundering for a method of escape from the predicament into which his folly had led him. He had no wish to pose as a freak in her eyes. Still, no solution offered itself.

"No," he said at length, "he never backed me. As a matter of fact, I am more of a physical instructor, now."

"Oh," she said, disappointedly, "I was going to gloat over Tommy. Physical instructor! Do you know father is looking for one for my two kid brothers? Why don't you apply?"

"Thanks," said Armitage, a bit ungraciously, "perhaps I shall."

Plainly the girl's interest in him was fast waning. Extremely chapfallen and deeply disgusted with himself, Armitage bowed, and, muttering something about looking after his luggage, withdrew.

CHAPTER III
PRINCE VASSILI KOLTSOFF

When Miss Wellington entered the cabin she found her mother in the same position in which she had left her, but her eyes were open, looking straight at the girl.

"Mother, I never knew you to do anything quite so *bourgeois* before." There was a gleam of mischief in her eyes. "Sleeping in a public place! You weren't sleeping, were you?"

"No, I was not," said her mother. "I have been thinking, planning."

"Oh, Prince Koltsoff!"

"Yes." Mrs. Wellington raised her hand languidly to her face. "He wrote he was coming to us this afternoon, direct from the Russian ambassador's at Bar Harbor. Did he not?"

"Yes, unless Miss Hatch was mistaken in what she said the other day."

"Miss Hatch," said the elder woman, "is one of the few secretaries I ever had who does not make mistakes. However, that is neither here nor there. Prince Koltsoff has been in Newport for a week."

"A week! The idea! Where? Not with the Van Antwerps?" Miss Wellington's eyes blazed with interest.

"No, not with any one that I was able to discover. But Clarie Pembroke, of the British legation, was driving from the Reading Room to the yacht club with your father the other day. He told me he was certain he saw Koltsoff standing on a side street near the Aquidneck."

"Why on earth did n't you tell me before?" cried the daughter. "What a delightful mystery!" She smiled with mischief. "Do you suppose after all he is some no-account? You know Russian princes are as numerous as Russian bears; they can be as great bounders and as indigent as Italian counts—"

"All of which you have heard me say quite frequently," interrupted Mrs. Wellington placidly. "Koltsoff is not pinchbeck. The Koltsoffs are an illustrious Russian family, and have been for years. I think I know my Almanach de Gotha. Why, Koltsoff is *aide-de-camp* to the Czar and has, I believe, estates in southern Russia. His father fought brilliantly in the Russo-Turkish War and gained the Cross of St. Anne; his great, or great-great-grandfather, I don't recall which, was a general of note of Catherine the Great's, and if certain intimate histories of that time are not wholly false, her rewards for his services were scandalously bestowed."

"No doubt," said the girl carelessly. "And Koltsoff?"

"A genuinely distinguished fellow. He was educated, of course, at the cadet school in St. Petersburg and during the Japanese War was with the Czar. I met him in London, last May, at Lord McEncroe's, as I have already told you, I think, and when he spoke of coming to America this summer I engaged him for August."

"It was rather farsighted of you," said the girl admiringly. "Newport needs some excitement this season. If he's anything like that last Russian who came here on a warship two years ago, you will shine as a benefactor, especially in the eyes of reporters."

Mrs. Wellington smiled grimly.

"The Grand Duke Ivan?"

"Yes; what a great bearded beast he was! I remember father bemoaning, when Ivan the Terrible departed, that there was no more of his favorite Planet brandy left in the Reading Room cellars."

Mrs. Wellington did not smile. She was eying her daughter curiously. "I want you and the Prince to become good friends," she said.

"That will depend upon whether he can gracefully explain his mysterious presence in Newport the past week," replied the girl laughingly. Suddenly her face grew grave. "What do you mean, mother?"

"Merely that I expect—that Prince Koltsoff hopes"—and under her daughter's steady gaze, she did something she had done but once or twice in her life—floundered and then paused.

The girl's lip curled, not mirthfully.

"Ah, I begin to understand," she said. "Prince Koltsoff's visit was conceived hardly in the nature of ordinary social emprise."

"Now, please don't go on, Anne," said the mother. "I have expressed nothing but a wish, have I? Wait until you know him."

"But you said Koltsoff had expressed a—a—"

"A hope, naturally. He saw Sargent's portrait of you in London."

"How romantic! I do not wonder you couldn't sleep, mother."

"Perhaps there were other reasons. Who was the man you ensnared outside?"

Miss Wellington laughed.

"Trust you, mother. He was very decent. He took me below and fed me hot biscuits and coffee. He said he was a prize fighter."

"A prize fighter!"

"He said so. But he was not telling the truth. He was awfully good looking and had a manner that one does not acquire. I am rather curious concerning him. You don't imagine he was Koltsoff, incog?"

Mrs. Wellington glanced witheringly at her.

"I imagine he may have been a reporter, Anne. Why are n't you more careful! There may come a time when your efforts to uphold your reputation for eccentricity and for doing the cleverly unexpected will react disagreeably."

It was the first time her mother had given her reason to believe that she shared in any way in the views concerning her which were prevalent among the younger set at least. The girl was not flattered.

"Mother, don't be so absurd," she said. "The only efforts I have ever made have been to lead a normal, human life and not a snobbish, affected one. Eccentric! The conditions under which we live are eccentric. My only desire is to be normal."

"Life is relative, you know," said Mrs. Wellington. "If you—" she glanced out the window and saw the Torpedo Station slipping past. "Why, we are almost in," she said. "Morgan, go out, please, and see if they have sent a motor for us."

The handful of passengers were filing down to the main deck and Mrs. Wellington, her daughter, and Emilia followed, where Morgan presently joined them with the announcement that she had not seen a Wellington car.

"*Peste!*" murmured Mrs. Wellington. "This is the last of Dawson if he has n't sent a car. I telegraphed last night."

"Telegrams have been known to go astray," suggested her daughter.

"Rot! So has Dawson," observed Mrs. Wellington.

It was only too plain when they crossed the gang plank that something or somebody had gone wrong. No automobile or horse-drawn vehicle bearing the Wellington insignia was at the landing. Having adjusted herself to the situation upon receiving her maid's report, Mrs. Wellington immediately signalled two of the less dingy hacks, entered one with her daughter, leaving the other for the maids.

"The Crags," she said, designating her villa to the hackman, who, touching his hat with the first sign of respect shown, picked up the reins. The driver, half turned in his seat to catch any conversation of an interesting nature, guided his horse to Thames Street and thence along that quaint, narrow thoroughfare toward Harbor Road.

Miss Wellington glanced at the driver and then looked at her mother solemnly.

"Do you suppose they will be up yet, mamma?" she said, with a sort of twanging nasal cadence.

Mrs. Wellington turned her head composedly toward the show windows of a store.

"I don't see why you won't say what you think, mamma," resumed the girl. "You know some of these Newporters, so the papers say, do not breakfast before eight o'clock."

"Eight o'clock!" There was an explosion of derisive mirth on the seat above them. "Ladies," the driver looked down with red cheeks and watery eyes, "if you expect to see 'Rome' Wellington's people, you 'd better drive round 'till eleven o'clock. And at that they won't have the sleep out of their eyes."

"Do these society people really sleep as late as that?" asked the girl.

The driver glanced at her a second.

"Aw, stop yer kiddin'," he said. "All I can say now is that if you try to wake 'em up now they 'll set the dogs on you."

"Very well, let them," interposed Mrs. Wellington. "Now drive on as quickly as possible—and no more talking, please."

The driver had a good look at her as she spoke. His round face became red and pale in turn and he clucked asthmatically to his horse.

"Good Lord," he muttered, "it's herself!"

But he had not much farther to go. Just as they turned into the Harbor Road, a Wellington car came up. The *mécanicien* had been losing no time, but when he caught sight of the Wellingtons he stopped within a distance which he prided himself was five feet less than any other living driver could have made it in, without breaking the car.

The footman was at the side of the hack in an instant and assisted the mother and daughter into the tonneau, which they entered in silence. Mrs. Wellington, in fact, did not speak until the car was tearing past the golf grounds. Here she turned to her daughter with a grim face.

"Anne," she said, "I've about made up my mind that you escaped being really funny with that impossible hackman."

"Yes, mother," said the girl, absently viewing the steadily rising roof of her home. "Our ideas of humor were ever alien. I wonder if Prince Koltsoff has arrived."

The Crags was one of the few Newport villas bordering on the sea, whose owners and architects had been sufficiently temperamental to take advantage of the natural beauties of its site. Upon huge black rocks, rising twenty-five or thirty feet, the house had been built. Windows on either side looked down upon the waters, ever shattering into white foam on half-hidden reefs, or rushing relentlessly into rocky, weed-hung fissures or black caverns. Sometimes in the autumn storms when the inrushing waves would bury deep the grim reefs off Bateman's Point and pile themselves on the very bulwarks of the island, the spray rattled against the windows of The Crags and made the place seem a part of the elemental fury.

In front of the house was an immense stretch of sward, bordered with box and relieved by a wonderful *parterre* and by walks and drives lined with blue hydrangeas. The stable, garage, and gardener's cottage were far to one side, all but their roofs concealed from the house and the roadway by a small grove of poplars.

Supplementing the processes of Nature by artificial means, Ronald Wellington had had a sort of fjord blasted out of the solid rock on the seaward side, as a passage for his big steam yacht, with steps leading from the house to the little wharf. Here lay the *Mayfair* when not in service; from the road you could see her mast tops, as though protruding from the ground. But now the *Mayfair* was down in a South Brooklyn shipyard; this thought, recurring to Mrs. Wellington, framed in her mind a mental picture of all that she had undergone as a result of that stupid blowing out of steam valves, which, by the way, had seriously scalded several of the engine-room staff and placed the keenest of edges upon her home-coming mood. No subject of nervous irritability, she. Incidents, affairs, persons, or things qualified to set the fibres of the average woman of her age tingling, were, with her, as the heat to steel; they tempered her, made her hard, keen, cold, resilient.

The butler, flanked by two or three men servants, met them at the door. Breakfast was served, he said. Prince Koltsoff, indeed, had already arrived, and had breakfasted.

"The Prince—" Mrs. Wellington checked herself and hurried into the breakfast room with inscrutable face. Her daughter followed, smiling broadly.

"The Prince seems to have anticipated us," she said.

Mrs. Wellington glanced at the alert-faced second man, who had just brought in the coffee, and compressed her lips into a straight line.

There was no conversation in the course of the short light breakfast. Anne went to her apartments, while Mrs. Wellington, after arising from the table, stood for a minute gazing from the window toward the polo grounds. Then slowly she mounted the stairs and, entering her boudoir, rang for her maid.

An hour and a half later, massaged, bathed, and robed in a dainty morning gown, Mrs. Wellington stepped into her "office," than which no one of her husband's many offices was more business-like, and seated herself at a large mahogany desk. Miss Hatch, her secretary, arose from a smaller desk with typewriter attachment and laid before her a number of checks for signing, bills rendered, invitations, and two bank books. Then she resumed her seat in silence.

Mrs. Wellington did not glance at the mass of matter. With a muttered "Thank you," she gazed thoughtfully at the row of white push buttons inlaid at her elbow. There were more than a dozen of them and they ranged from the pantry to the kitchen, from the garage to the stable. By means of them the mistress of The Crags kept in touch with nearly fifty servants. Here at her desk she could plan her campaigns, lay counter mine against mine, plan stratagems, and devise ideas. Her superiority over those who sought, or had sought in the past, to rival her lay in the fact that she could devise, outline, and execute her projects without assistance. A former secretary with some degree of literary talent had, upon dismissal, written up that office and its genius for a Sunday newspaper, and several hundred thousand good people, upon reading it, had marvelled at the tremendous means employed to such trivial ends.

But after all, who shall say what is trivial in this world and what is not? Let it rest with the assertion that in any other sphere, business, sociology, charity, Belle Wellington's genius would have carried her as far as in that domain wherein she had set her endeavors. As to charity, for that matter, she had given a mountain recluse, a physician, five hundred thousand dollars with which to found a tuberculosis sanitarium, and—but those were things which not even her friends knew and concerning which, therefore, we should remain silent.

Slowly she leaned forward and pressed a button. Mrs. Stetson, the housekeeper, soon appeared.

"Good-morning, Mrs. Stetson," she said. "Prince Koltsoff seems to have anticipated us." She suddenly remembered she had utilized her daughter's expression, and bit her lips. "When did he arrive?"

"He came last night in the French ambassador's carriage."

"Last night!" Mrs. Wellington glanced at her secretary. "Will you bring my engagement book, please." This in hand, she turned the pages hastily, then put it down.

"There has been some mistake. He was not to come to us until luncheon to-day. Was M. Renaud with him?"

"Yes, Mrs. Wellington, but he did not stay. The Prince seemed to know he was not expected. He apologized profusely, but said that events had brought him here a day early and trusted there was no inconvenience. He did not dine, but spent the evening in the smoking-room, writing. He sent two cable despatches by Parker."

"Um-m, *dégagé*, even for a Russian," said Mrs. Wellington. "And he arose early?"

"Very early. He asked Mr. Dawson for a car to go to the village at half after six."

Mrs. Wellington almost revealed her intense interest.

"Ah, to the village," she said. "Did he say—did he explain the reasons for his early trip?"

"No, but Parker told Mr. Dawson he stopped at the telegraph office."

"Where is the Prince now?"

"He is in the morning-room, writing."

"Thank you, Mrs. Stetson."

As the housekeeper left, Mrs. Wellington pressed another button, summoning the superintendent.

"Mr. Dawson," she said, "you received my wire last night that the *Mayfair* had broken down and that we were taking the midnight train from New York?"

"Yes, Mrs. Wellington."

"And you thought the Prince was going to meet us with that car? That was the reason for your failure to follow my instructions?"

"Yes, madame, thank you. I supposed Prince Koltsoff knew you were coming and that he had ordered the car to meet you. When this proved wrong I sent Rimini. I am glad he was not late."

"He was late. He met us, packed in a miserable hack. Hereafter I must insist upon strict compliance with my wishes. Do not assume things, please. Am I quite clear? Thank you." Mrs. Wellington turned from him and pressed still another button. In a moment the tutor of her two sons, Ronald, sixteen years old, and Royal, twelve, stood before her. He was a Frenchman, whose facial expression did not indicate that his duties had fallen in the pleasantest of places.

"Good-morning, M. Dumois. Where are my sons?" She spoke in French.

"They attended a party at Bailey's Beach and remained the night with Master Van Antwerp."

"How have they been?"

"Very well, thank you, except—"

"Except?"

"I found Master Ronald smoking a cigarette in the smoking-room yesterday."

Mrs. Wellington dashed a note on her pad.

"Thank you," she said in her soft tone of dismissal.

"Lest Miss Wellington forget, you might, on your way, remind her, in my name, not to meet Prince Koltsoff until I receive him at luncheon."

She turned to the mass of correspondence on her desk and selected for first reading a long telegram from her husband, who, when he sent it, was speeding eastward through the Middle West in his special car. She laid it down with a faraway smile in her eyes. She loved and admired her big husband, who did things, knocked men's heads together, juggled railroads and steamships in either hand. And this love and admiration, in whatever she had done or wherever placed, had always been as twin flaming angels guarding her with naked swords.

Presently she turned to her secretary and dictated a statement concerning the arrival of Prince Koltsoff, who he was, and a list of several of the entertainments given in his honor.

"You might call Mr. Craft at the Newport *Herald* office and give him this," she said.

Half an hour was spent in going over accounts, signing checks, auditing bills, and the like, and then with a sigh she arose and passed into her dressing-room. Ordinarily she would have dressed for the beach or the Casino. But to-day she threw herself on a couch in her boudoir and closed her eyes. But she did not sleep.

M. Dumois, hastening to comply with his mistress' command, failed to find the girl in her apartments. At the moment, indeed, that Emilia was informing the tutor that the girl had left for the stables, Miss Wellington from a corner of the hall was gazing interestedly at the Prince, who sat with his profile toward her. He was bending over a table upon which was spread a parchment drawing. The sunlight fell full upon him. He was not at all unprepossessing. Tall and slim, with waist in and well-padded shoulders, his blonde hair and Van Dyck bead, long white eyelashes, darker brows, and glittering blue eyes, he was the very type of the aristocratic Muscovite.

As the girl looked she saw his lips part and his teeth glisten. He half arose, leaned forward, and smote the chart.

Miss Wellington hurried down the hall and out of the house.

"Prince Koltsoff," she murmured, as she swung down the path to the stable, "I would give worlds to know what you 're up to. I definitely place you as a rascal. But oh, such a romantically picturesque one!"

CHAPTER IV
THE TAME TORPEDO

That night Lieutenant Armitage, in a marine's drab shirt and overalls, stood among a silent group of mechanics on a pier near the Goat Island lighthouse. A few hundred feet out lay a small practice torpedo boat, with the rays of a searchlight from the bridge of the parent ship of the First Flotilla resting full upon her.

Suddenly Armitage leaned forward. When he straightened there came a dull report, a lurid flash of light, and with a sharp whirring sound a model torpedo about half the regulation size, leaped through the darkness and with a clear parting of the waters disappeared. A green Very star cleaved the night. Intense silence followed. One second, two seconds, elapsed and then from the practice boat out in the harbor a red star reared. Armitage turned to the master mechanic at his side.

"Bully!" he said. "I aimed at least twenty feet wide of the *Dumont*. The magnetos fetched her. But wait—"

In the glare of the searchlight he could see they had lowered a boat and were recovering the torpedo. He saw a group of young officers gather about it as it was hauled aboard, and then in a minute or so the red and green Ardois lights began to wink. As Armitage watched with straining eyes he spelled the message as it came, letter by letter.

"A fair hit. But the wrong end struck."

The *Dumont* was sufficiently near the pier for the message to have been shouted. But tests of new torpedoes are not to be shouted about. Armitage discharged a white star from his pistol, the signal to come in for the night, and walked toward the shops.

"You may turn in," he said to the men. "I have a good night's work, alone, ahead of me."

"She should not have struck with her stern, sir," said a short, squat man, hurrying to Armitage's side. He spoke with a strong accent and passed as a Lithuanian. His expert knowledge of electricity as well as his skill in making and mending apparatus had caused Armitage to intrust him with much of the delicate work on the model, as well as on the torpedo of regular size, based on the model, now in course of construction.

His was a position of peculiar importance. As the blue-prints of the invention, from which detailed plans were worked, passed into the shops, they came into the hands of this man, who, thus, many times in the course of the day had the working prints of the controlling mechanism in his exclusive possession.

For some reason that he could not explain, all this shot through Armitage's mind as the man spoke.

"No, Yeasky, it should not. But I'll fix that. By the way, how long—No matter, I shan't need you any more to-night, Yeasky."

As he entered the shop the storekeeper was leaving. He nodded to the officer.

"What luck, Lieutenant Armitage?"

"Fair, the wrong end hit first. I think the regulation size would have worked all right. At all events, I'll study it out to-night."

He paused. Then as the storekeeper stepped past him he called him back.

"Mr. Jackson, I may be silly, but I've been a bit worried of late. You keep a close eye on the record of parts, don't you?"

"Yes, indeed, sir, I go over it every night."

"Do you ever actually go over the parts to see that they tally with the records? What I mean is, important parts might be missing, although the daily record might be so juggled as to make it appear they were not."

"By George!" exclaimed the storekeeper, "I never have done that. I'll begin to-morrow."

"Thanks, I should if I were you. Good-night."

Armitage passed into the shop and switched on an electric light over a long pine table in the centre of the apartment. Then he went to the safe, opened it, and returned to the table with an armful of rolled parchment and specifications. These he spread out and thereafter, while the night waned, he was lost to the world and its affairs.

Briefly, Armitage had invented a torpedo, whose steering was so controlled by delicate magnetos, that while ordinarily proceeding in the line of aim, if such aim, through the movement of the vessel aimed at, or through some other cause, should result in a miss, the effect of the steel hull of the objective ship on the delicate magnetos of the Armitage torpedo would be such as to cause a change in the course of the deadly missile, and have her go directly toward the vessel and even follow her.

Armitage, whose mechanical genius had marked him while at the Academy as a man of brilliant possibilities, had developed his idea in the course of several years, and when it was perfected in his mind he had gone to the Chief of Ordnance at Washington and laid the matter before him in all its details. The chief at once gave the lie to the theory long current that the Department was averse to progress along whatever line, by expressing unqualified delight. He had Armitage ordered to the Torpedo Station at Newport to carry on experiments forthwith, and instructed the superintendent of the station to give the inventor every facility for carrying on his work. Two months had already elapsed and the work was at the stage when a destroyer and a practice torpedo boat had been detached from regular duty and placed at his exclusive service.

The Government was deeply interested in the progress of the work, and had shown it in many ways. The significance of such a torpedo in any war in which the country might become involved was patent. Rumors more or less vague had leaked, as such things do, to foreign war offices, and there was not a naval *attaché* at Washington but had received imperative orders to leave nothing undone by which the exact nature of the torpedo and its qualifications might be ascertained. But neither Armitage nor the Department had any idea of permitting the slightest information regarding the invention to escape.

All matters connected with the invention had been carried forward with the utmost secrecy, while the pedigree of every man employed in the work had been investigated carefully. All but Yeasky were native-born mechanics, and he had come from a great electrical plant in New Jersey with highest recommendations as to character and ability.

The sound of bells ringing for early mass was floating across the water from the city, when Armitage, with a deep breath of relief, walked from the table and threw himself with legs outstretched into a chair.

"No," he said with a triumphant grimace, "there will be no mistake next time. There was not a single fault in the model except—" He suddenly started bolt upright and looked about him. Then he settled back laughing. "A fine state of nerves," he added, "when I am afraid to talk to myself."

He arose with the pleasing design of enjoying a cold tub and a shave on board the destroyer, the *D'Estang*, but the idea of pumping his water did not accord with his mood.

He walked over to Billy Harrison's house. Billy commanded the First Flotilla and, being married, had quarters on the reservation. A drowsy servant answered the bell. She said that the Harrisons were still asleep.

"Well, never mind," said Armitage, chuckling, "I'll be back later."

Instead of going away he went around to the side, seized a handful of gravel, and threw it into an open second story window. He could hear it rattle against the wall and floor. A short silence followed and Armitage was about to pick up more gravel when a girl in a green and white dressing-gown appeared.

"Jack Armitage!" she cried, falling to her knees, so that only her head rose above the sill. "What on earth do you want now?"

"Why, hello, Letty," laughed Armitage. "Where's Billy?"

"He's here, sleeping. What do you mean by throwing stones into my window?"

"I want to talk to Billy," said Armitage.

"He's asleep, I tell you. What do you want?"

"Well, I want to borrow your tub and Billy's razors."

"Why didn't you say so? Ring the bell and come right up. I'll have some towels put in. And say, Jack, really—"

"What?"

"I hope you drown, waking me this way. And, Jack, stay to breakfast, won't you, like a good chap?"

Which Jack did. An hour or so later, fresh and cool and with that comfortable feeling which follows a well-cooked Navy breakfast,—bacon and eggs,—his pipe sending blue clouds into the sparkling air, Armitage walked over to the torpedo boat slips. Across the harbor lay the city, bathed in golden sunshine, the tree-clad streets rising tier by tier to the crown, Bellevue Avenue. His gaze wandered seaward and for the first time since sunset he thought of Anne Wellington. Would he ever see her again? What was she doing now, he wondered. No doubt she would attend service at Trinity; many of the cottagers did. He, too, would go to church there. He had not been lately; it would do him good, he told himself.

Thus thinking, he stepped aboard the black, ominous, oily *D'Estang*, made his way aft and clambered down the companion ladder. There was the usual Sunday morning gathering of young officers from the boats of the flotilla. The smoke, mainly from pipes—three weeks having elapsed since pay day—was thick, and an excited argument, not over speeding records, or coal consumption, but over the merits of an English vaudeville actor who had appeared the week before at Freebody Park, was in progress.

"Hello, Jack," said a tall dark officer in spotless white uniform, "how's the tame torpedo this morning?"

"Fine, fine, Blackie," grinned Armitage. "How's that tin cup, misnamed the *Jefferson*, to-day?"

"Did n't eat out of your hand last night, did she?" observed Tommy Winston of the *Adams*, attired in blue trousers and a flannel shirt.

"No, but she will," said Armitage.

"No doubt," replied Winston with his quaint Southern drawl. "Look here, Jackie, where you going this morning, all dressed up in gorgeous cits clothes?"

"To church," replied Armitage, "to Trinity; any one want to go with me?" he asked, ignoring the derisive chorus.

There was a moment's silence and then Bob Black looked at him quizzically.

"Does any one want to go with you?" he jeered. "Who 's the girl?"

"I wonder—But seriously, I have never been to the service there and since the Wellingtons asked me to drop into their pew any Sunday, I—"

"The Wellingtons!" exclaimed Thornton of the submarine *Polyp*. "You don't mean the Ronald Wellingtons?"

"No, I don't mean any Wellingtons at all. I was joking. Why?"

"Then you did n't hear of Thornton's run in with them last week?" said Winston. "That's so, you were in Washington."

"What was it, Joe?" asked Armitage, turning to Thornton.

"Why, nothing much. Two of my men were arrested last Thursday for assaulting the Wellington kids. It seems they were walking past Bailey's Beach and the youngsters bombarded them with clam shells and gravel. It would have been all right, but one of the shells caught Kelly on the cheek and cut him. The men didn't do a thing but jump over that hedge into the holy of holies, gather in the young scions, and knock their heads together."

"You don't say! What happened then?"

"They were arrested and the chief sent over here. I got the men's story and then called the Wellingtons' house on the telephone. Mrs. Wellington's secretary answered. I told her who I was and that I wanted to talk about the case with some one in authority. She asked me to hold the wire and in a few seconds the queen herself was holding pleasant converse with yours truly.

"'You say the men are under your command?' she said.

"I replied, 'Even so.' Then she gave me the name of her lawyer and said Kelly and Burke would be prosecuted on every charge that could be brought to bear."

Armitage laughed.

"Trust her! What did you say?"

"I got hot under the collar right away, then. 'Mrs. Wellington,' I said, 'my men were not to blame. If they were I should not have called you on the 'phone. But your sons threw shells and cut one of them. They were punished, and justly. And I now advise you I am going to have counter warrants issued against your boys if the charge is pressed in court to-day!' Just like that.

"Her voice came crisp. 'You say my sons were at fault? Have you any proof of that?'

"I came back in a second. 'I have sufficient proof to convince even your lawyer.'

"'Very well,' she said. 'Then do it. I shall direct him to see you at once. If what you say is true we will of course take no further action.'

"The case was dropped all right."

"Bully for you," said Armitage. "My Lady evidently has a sense of justice."

"Here 's a paragraph," said Winston, holding up a local paper, "which says that a physical instructor is wanted at The Crags. They are going to prepare for future engagements with our men, evidently."

"Well, let me tell you that Anne Wellington is a corker," observed Black suddenly.

"Anne Wellington?" said Armitage ingenuously.

"Yes," continued Black, "the daughter. I saw her at the Casino the other day. She was joshing some little old rooster who was trying to play tennis and she had him a mile up in the air. She 's beautiful, too. That's more than you can say of most of these alleged society beauties."

"Which reminds me," said Armitage, glancing at his watch, "that I am due for church. Come on, Joe," he added, "be a good chap."

Thornton in the goodness of his nature arose.

"All right," he said. "I'm game." Thornton had been a star full-back at Annapolis when Armitage was an All America end, and he would have gone to worse places than church for his old messmate.

Nowadays he spent his time in sinking the *Polyp* among the silt on the harbor bottom, for which work his crew received several dollars apiece, extra pay, for each descent. Thornton received not even glory, unless having gone to the floor of Long Island Sound with a President of the United States be held as constituting glory.

CHAPTER V
AT TRINITY

Old Trinity rests on the hillside, serene in the afterglow of its one hundred and eighty-four years. The spotless white walls, the green blinds, the graceful Colonial spire, are meetly set in an environment which strikes no note of dissonance. On either side are quaint, narrow streets, lined with decent door-yards and houses almost as old as the church. Within the cool interior the cottagers, and representatives of a native aristocracy—direct descendants of the English of the sixteenth and seventeenth centuries, who are so conservative, so proudly, scornfully aloof, that one would doubt they existed at all, were it not for their stately homes in the older sections of the city, where giant elms keep watch and ward over eave and column and dormer window, where hydrangeas sweep the doorstep, and faun and satyr, rough hewn, peer through the shrubbery—sit primly in the box-like pews with the preacher towering above them under the white sounding board.

The church was not half filled when Armitage and Thornton arrived, but a double line of visitors were standing in the rear aisle. Armitage caught the eye of one of the ushers and beckoned to him. But that frock-coated, austere personage coldly turned his glance elsewhere and Armitage had started forward to enlist his attention in a manner that would admit of no evasion when his companion caught him by the sleeve, chuckling.

"Look here, old chap," he whispered, "you have to wait until they know how many pew-holders are going to be absent. This is n't a theatre."

Armitage turned his head to reply, when a rustling of skirts sounded behind him and Thornton punched him in the ribs.

"The Wellington bunch," he whispered, "and the Russian they have captured."

It was a fine entry, as circus folks say. First came Mrs. Wellington in a simple but wonderfully effective embroidered linen gown, then her two sons, likely enough boys, and then Anne Wellington with Prince Koltsoff. She almost touched Armitage as she passed; the skirt of her lingerie frock swished against his ankles and behind she left, not perfume, but an intangible essence suggestive, somehow, of the very personality of the cool, beautiful, lithe young woman. As Armitage turned in response to Thornton's prod in the ribs, he met her eyes in full. But she gave no sign of recognition, and of course Armitage did not.

The Wellingtons had two pews, according to the diagram on the rear seats, and as Armitage followed the party with his eyes, he saw the mother, her daughter, and the Prince enter one, the boys seating themselves in the stall ahead.

In the meantime the congregation had assembled in large numbers and the body of the church as well as the side aisles were comfortably filled. From time to time the ushers, with machine-like precision, took one or two persons from the patiently waiting line of non-pew-holders and escorted them to seats, a proceeding which began to irritate Armitage, seeing which Thornton grinned and observed, *sotto voce*, that one might worship here only at the price of patience.

"It's the sheep and the goats, Jack," he whispered.

"I don't know about the sheep, but we 're the goats, all right," replied Armitage, "and I for one am going to beat it right now."

He had started for the door and Thornton was following when an usher hurrying up touched him on the shoulder, bowing unctuously.

"Miss Wellington," he said, "asked to have you gentlemen shown into the Wellington pew."

His voice clearly indicated that he felt he had been neglecting angels unawares, to say nothing of a desire to atone for his indiscretion.

The young men nodded as indifferently as the situation seemed to require and followed the man to the stall in which the boys were seated, who pushed in hospitably enough and then returned to their prayer books.

It must be said that two handsomer men, or men better constructed physically, never sat together in old Trinity; Thornton a perfect, brawny, rangy blonde; Armitage, shorter, better knit, perhaps, with shoulders just as broad, and short crinkling brown hair surmounting his squarely defined, sun-browned features.

The sermon was somewhat revolutionary, but Anne Wellington paid but slight attention. While the good clergyman warned his hearers of the terrible reckoning which must eventually come from neglect by the upper classes of the thousands born month after month in squalor and reared amid sordid, vicious surroundings, the girl's eyes rarely wandered from the two men in front of her. It was uplifting, conducive to healthful, normal emotions to look at them, and such emotions were exactly what she needed.

Radiating, as it were, from Prince Koltsoff was an influence she did not like. On the contrary, feeling its power, she had begun to fear it. He attracted her peculiarly. She could not quite explain the sensation; it was indefinable, vague, but palpable nevertheless. Then he was high in the Russian nobility, upon terms of friendship with the Czar, a prominent figure in the highest society of European capitals. His wife would at once take a position which any girl might covet. True, she would probably be unhappy with him after the first bloom of his devotion, but then she might not. She might be able to hold him. Miss Wellington flattered herself that she could. And if not—well, she would not be the first American girl to pocket that loss philosophically and be content with the contractual profits that remained. A Russian princess of the highest patent of nobility—there was a thrill in that thought, which, while it did not dominate her, might eventually have that effect.

At all events, she found it not at all objectionable that Prince Koltsoff was apparently enamoured of her. Of this she was quite certain. He had a way of looking his devotion. His luminous blue eyes were wonderful in their expressiveness. They could convey almost any impression in the gamut of human emotions, save perhaps kindliness, and among other things they had told her he loved her.

That was flattering, but the trouble was that so often his eyes made her blush confusedly without any reason more tangible than that he was looking at her.

Anne Wellington was as thoroughly feminine as any girl that ever lived, and had always gloried in her sex. She had never wished she were a man. Still there is a happy mean for every normal American girl, and already she had begun to wonder if the Prince was ever going to forget that she was a woman and treat her as an ordinary human being, with the question of sex in the abstract at least.

Yet on the other hand there was that thrill which she could not deny. She felt as though she were living through an experience and was curious as to the outcome. With her, curiosity was a challenge. Withal, for the first time in her life, she was afraid of herself. And so she found her study of the two young men in front of her wholesome and antiseptic, as Kipling says.

As the preacher suddenly paused and then demanded in ringing tones what those of the upper classes intended to do about the situation which he had been eloquently portraying, a portly old gentleman whose breath would have proclaimed that he had had a cocktail at the Reading Room before service, heaved a loud, hopeless sigh. She saw Thornton nudge Armitage with his shoulder and the replying grin wrinkle Jack's face. Swiftly her eyes turned sideways to the Prince. He was sitting half turned in the seat regarding her with worshipping gaze. She thrilled under the contrast;

compared to the men in front of her, Koltsoff was a mere—yes, a mere monkey. What did he take her for, a school girl?

Filled with her emotions, she impulsively opened a little gold pencil with which she had been toying and wrote rapidly upon one of the blank pages of her hymnal, which later she surreptitiously tore out. When the service was ended and Armitage and Thornton with slight bows of acknowledgment passed into the aisle, the girl leaned toward the younger of her two brothers.

"Muck," she said, "be a good chap and give this note to the dark-haired man who sat next to you. Do it nicely, now, Muck, so no one will see you. I'll pay you back for it. Hurry."

Muck, who adored his sister, nodded and worked his way through the departing worshippers until he came up with Armitage. He pushed the note into the young officer's hand and as Armitage started in surprise the boy nodded his head knowingly.

"Say nothing," he warned.

So well had the boy carried it through that not even Thornton observed the incident. Armitage said nothing to enlighten him, but spread the page open in his hand as though he had taken a memorandum from his pocket.

It was as follows:

MY DEAR MR. PRIZE FIGHTER—

I was really serious the other day about your applying for the position of physical instructor. My small brothers were mauled by sailors the other day and mother is keen for some one who will teach them how to obtain their revenge some day. You might see mother or her secretary any morning after eleven. I have spoken to both about you.

A. V. D. W.

Twice Armitage read it and then he folded it carefully and placed it in his breast pocket, a curious smile playing over his face.

"We think," he said, addressing himself under his breath, as was his wont upon occasion, "we think we shall keep this for future reference. For we never know how soon we may need a job."

It has been observed ere this how many truths are sometimes spoken in jest.

CHAPTER VI
AN ENCOUNTER WITH A SPY

At the door of the church, Thornton met a retired rear admiral and his wife, whose daughter he knew. So he paused and was affably solicitous whether they found the glorious August weather conducive to their general well-being. Armitage bowed and drew to one side, just as the Wellington party passed out into the churchyard and walked down the path to their motor panting at the curb.

The Prince helped Mrs. Wellington and her daughter into the tonneau with easy grace and then motioned the two boys to precede him. He was not at all bad looking, Armitage decided. Tall and rather wasp-waisted he was, nevertheless well set up, and his tailor easily might have left a pound or so of padding out of the blue jacket and still have avoided the impression that the Prince was narrow-backed. His manner certainly bore every impress of courtly breeding and the insolence of rank was by no means lacking, as Armitage learned the next instant, when a man whose back was strangely familiar, suddenly appeared at Koltsoff's side and, with hat in hand, essayed to address him.

Armitage, watching eagerly, saw the Russian's form stiffen, saw his eyes, as cold and steady as steel discs, fix themselves unseeingly over the man's head, who bowed awkwardly and turning hurriedly with a flushed face, stumbled against a horse post.

A low exclamation leaped from Armitage's lips. He hesitated just an instant and then fairly ran out of the doorway and down the path to the street. He caught up with the fellow before he had gone a hundred feet. Looking back to see that the Wellington car had gone, he touched him on the arm.

"Look here, Yeasky," he said, as the man wheeled in nervous haste, "who was that chap you spoke to at that motor car?"

Yeasky hesitated a moment and then looked the officer full in the eyes.

"I do not know," he said; "I thought it was Commander Harris. I was going to ask him about those coils which have not come yet. When I found I mistook, I was ashamed."

Armitage returned the electrician's gaze for a second. He was at a loss. There was a slight resemblance between Harris and the Prince, to be sure. Then, suddenly, as he recalled the incident at the Grand Central Station and his fears of the previous evening, a wave of anger swept over him and he thrust his face belligerently toward the workman, the muscles of his right shoulder calling nervously for action.

"Yeasky," he said, "you are lying. Who do you think you are up against,—a child?" He shook his finger in the man's face. "Now quick; tell me what business you had with that man." Yeasky drew himself up with an air of offended dignity not altogether compatible with his putative station in life. Armitage noticed it and pressed on.

"Do you hear?" he said in a low tense voice. He was already past saving; he had never been a diplomat. "Hurry up, speak, or I 'll knock your Polack head off."

Before the man could reply, Thornton, who had hurried up, interposed.

"What's the matter, Jack? Did this gentleman have the misfortune to demand all of the sidewalk?"

Armitage replied over his shoulder.

"You go along, Joe, and leave this to me. I saw this man trying to talk to that Russian Prince—and he's employed on confidential work in the shops."

"I know, Jack," said Thornton soothingly, placing his hand on Armitage's shoulder. "But it is n't policy to get into a street fight about it, you know, old chap."

"It wouldn't be a fight," began Armitage sneeringly. He turned suddenly toward Yeasky. "I have been pestered and worried for a week now. I know I was shadowed in New York. Now that I 've a clue I am not going to let go of it."

"Of course not," said Thornton, "but you don't want to go off half cocked. Remember you were up all last night. Just heave to a second. Has anything happened at the shops?"

"No," said Armitage, cooling a bit, "not that I know of. But this fellow's doing inside work here on the torpedo and I saw him talking to that Russian."

"Talking?"

"I mean he tried to. He says he thought the man was Harris, and he wanted to ask him about some coils. That was too fishy for me."

"Did the Prince talk to him?"

"No; snubbed, ignored him."

"Oh," smiled Thornton. "Well, I say, Jack, honestly I think you might be wrong. Harris does suggest that Prince chap; I thought so in church. Of course you can decide about this fellow's future in the shops, as you think best. But you really can't do anything here."

"I suppose you are right," said Armitage reluctantly. He nodded toward the man.

"Yeasky, if you are straight, meet me at the storekeeper's office at three o'clock this afternoon. I hope by that hour to be in a position to apologize to you. In the meantime," his good nature, as with all persons of warm temperament, speedily returning, "if I have wronged you, I am sorry."

"You have wronged me," replied Yeasky. "But I understand your feelings. I shall certainly meet you at three o'clock."

"Three, sharp." And Armitage, with Thornton's arm drawn through his, walked down the street.

Yeasky stood watching them for a second and then clapping his hand to his pocket a smile spread slowly over his face. He followed the two stalwart officers for a few steps and paused irresolutely. Then, without further hesitancy, he walked rapidly to Spring Street and thence to the Hotel Aquidneck, where he entered the telephone booth. When he emerged he paid toll on five charges.

This done he went into the writing-room and called for a small piece of wrapping paper and twine. When it came he took from his pocket a bulky, heavy object, done up in a newspaper. Without removing this, he wrapped it neatly in the manila paper, bound it securely, and addressed it in printed letters. He sat for a moment looking thoughtfully at the package. Then he drew a sheet of note paper toward him, cut off the hotel heading and dipped his pen in the ink.

He began:

Vassili Andreyvitch, I am sending you by messenger as you instructed over the telephone, the vital part. There is nothing more to do and I leave Newport this hour, for excellent reasons. I was seen trying to address you this morning, so watch out.

Yeasky read this last sentence again and then the thought that he would be confirmed as a bungler in his superior's mind occurred to him. He inked out the sentence, muttering that Koltsoff must take care of himself, as he had had to do, and then resumed his writing.

When you get this I shall be in parts unknown. I begin to fear I am suspect. You can reach me care of Garlock, Boston, to-night, and Blavatsky, Halifax, on Wednesday. On that day I go via the Dominion Line to England and thence to the secret police office in St. Petersburg. Forgive, I pray, this haste, but I have done all there is to be done. I accept your congratulations—and now having no desire to pose as the centre of a diplomatic situation, I go—Au Revoir.

He called a messenger, despatched the package and the letter, and within half an hour was in a trolley car bound for Fall River.

CHAPTER VII
MISS WELLINGTON CROSSES SWORDS WITH A DIPLOMAT

As Koltsoff, who had been summoned to the telephone, returned to the morning-room of the Wellington house, he looked about him with a triumphant gleam in his eye. He loved the part he was playing in Newport, a part, by the way, which he had played not always ineptly in other quarters of the world. He loved mystery; and like many Russians, the fact that he was a part, the centre, of any project of international emprise, questionable or otherwise, was to him the very breath of life. Innuendo, political intrigue, diplomatic tergiversation—in all these he was a master. Nor did he neglect the color, the atmosphere. Here was his weakness. Vague hints, a significant smile here, a shrug there, a lifting of the brows—all temptations too great for him to resist, had at times the effect of setting his effectiveness in certain ventures partially if not completely at naught. Temperamental proclivities are better for their absence among the component elements of a diplomat's mental equipment.

He had now in contemplation a genuine *affaire du coeur*. Thus far, everything had gone well. He sighed the sigh of perfect self-adjustment, sign of a mind agreeably filled, and stretching out his legs picked up a volume of Bourget. He fingered the pages idly for a few minutes and then laid it aside and half closed his eyes, nodding and smiling placidly. He sat thus when Anne Wellington entered.

Rays of sunlight, flooding through the windows glorified the girl, made her radiant as a spirit. And the Prince, who, if genuine in few things, was at least a true worshipper of beauty, was exalted. He arose, bowed slightly, and then advanced with wonderful charm of manner.

"My dear Miss Wellington," he murmured, "you come as the morning came, so fresh and so beautiful."

"How polite of you," smiled the girl. "If our men were so facile—" she opened one of the French windows and stepped out on the veranda, looking over the restless waters to the yellow-green Narragansett hills.

"So facile?" asked Koltsoff, following.

"—So facile in their compliments, I am afraid we should grow to be unbearable." She paused and smiled brightly at the Prince. "And yet women of your country are not so; at least those whom I have met."

"That," replied the Russian, turning his eyes full upon hers, "is because we are discriminating, if, as you say, facile."

Anne flushed and laughed and then dropped lightly into a big wicker chair, conscious that Koltsoff had not withdrawn his gaze. She leaned forward and flicked her skirts over her ankles, nervously pulled a stray wisp of hair from her neck. Then she slowly met the eyes of the man standing at her side and propounded an inquiry having to do with nothing less banal than his views of America thus far. Prince Koltsoff tossed his head and thus threw off the question. This amused the girl.

"Really," she said, "don't you find a remarkable resemblance between Newport and the Isle of Wight? At least—pray sit down, won't you—I have found them very like."

Prince Koltsoff seated himself daintily in a chair at her side and his face lit under the influence of a triumphant thought.

"You speak of the Isle of Wight, Miss Wellington, neglecting one great point of difference. Newport possesses you. They are, therefore, to me, totally different." He waved one hand slightly and drew his cigarette case from his pocket with the other, glancing at the girl.

"Oh, certainly," she said, "please smoke."

"But the difference," pursued Koltsoff, "don't you think it remarkable that it should be so apparent to me?"

"Do you know," she said, glancing down at the toes of her slippers, "I am not sufficiently inter—" She stopped abruptly and shrugged her shoulders. "Oh, let us be impersonal, Prince Koltsoff, it is so much nicer."

The Prince frowned.

"But, please," he said, "I wish to be personal. Am I at fault if I find you interesting? Character is one of my most absorbing studies. I am rather scientific. I see sometimes in persons, more than others see who are not so observing, or scientific, as you please." He lit his cigarette. "In you, for instance."

Miss Wellington, caught off her guard, started. The flash of a smile crossed Koltsoff's face. His inclination to show off, to reveal his cleverness, triumphed over his small supply of tact.

"I! 'For instance'! What do you mean, Prince Koltsoff?"

"Why, this morning at your church. As hidden depths of character reveal themselves—" the Prince raised his eyes. "That billet—shall we say *billet doux*?" He raised his shoulders and let them fall slowly. "Women! Ah! most interesting!"

For a moment Anne maintained her expression of mild inquiry, but within she was mentally perturbed. Irritation succeeded and she resolved to punish him for his insolence, even at the risk of indiscretion.

"You see many things, do you not?" she said, mockingly.

"Yes," he agreed, following her lead, "I see very, very many things. It is a faculty. It has been most useful."

"I should not flatter myself that I alone possessed that faculty, Prince Koltsoff, if I were you." She leaned forward, her chin upon her hand and gazed thoughtfully seaward. "I also am not sightless."

She leaned back in her chair languidly and watched the Prince's change of expression with open amusement.

"So, you have found it worth while to observe me? I am quite flattered." His impression that she had discharged a random shot grew with his words and soon became conviction. "I thank you."

Anne laughed.

"You are quite welcome to all you received—in the way of my interest in you. It is only fair, however, to suggest that we do not always obtain information concerning our friends—'you, for instance,'" she mimicked him perfectly, "through general observation. Some things may obtrude themselves, don't you know, in the most—what was your word? Oh, yes, 'scientific'—the most unscientific manner."

The Prince looked at her intently.

"You are speaking in innuendo, Miss Wellington," he replied. His tone was low and rapid.

"I am speaking quite truthfully, Prince Koltsoff," she said, with an inflection of emphasis.

"How could I doubt that!" He bowed. "That is why I am certain that you will be more explicit."

"There, you really don't insist, do you?" He saw a malicious light in her eyes.

"My dear Miss Wellington, most assuredly I do insist. I—I beg your pardon—I do more: I demand. Certainly it is my right."

Anne was all mischief now.

"Very well, then, I am able to inform you that you were in Newport incog, several days before you came to us. Do you conceive my right to call this to your attention, in view of the fact that you told us you had just arrived from Washington?"

Prince Koltsoff, as though absorbing her meaning, sat motionless, gazing at her steadily. Then he leaned forward and placed his hand on hers for a moment.

"Miss Wellington, you have done well. I pride myself on some diplomatic experience. You have negotiated your *coup* in a manner worthy of a De Staël. You would adorn the service. I wonder if you realize the possibilities of your future in an international sphere. To you I have no fear of talking. Listen, then."

Unconsciously the girl bent toward him.

"I am a diplomat," he continued. "There are things which—" he lifted his brows. "Newport—the French ambassador is here; the German ambassador is at Narragansett Pier, and I—who knows where I am—and why? But some day—"

He drew a long breath. "Rest content now, Miss Wellington, that I am progressing toward the gratitude of my Government; you shall hear more. Of course," he waved his hand, "I have spoken for your ear."

"Of course," said Miss Wellington, calmly, but inwardly curious nevertheless. "Should you care to walk to the stables?"

He nodded and then walking beside her he continued impulsively:

"I am not a soldier, Miss Wellington. But all victories are not won on the battlefields. The art—one of the arts—of diplomacy is to bring on war, if war must be, when you are ready and your adversaries are not. There are other functions. Let it be so. I but observe that one may wield things other than the sword and better than the sword, to serve one's country."

"I quite believe you." There was enthusiasm in her voice. "You may never expect the glory of the soldier, and yet how glorious the work must be! The matching of wits instead of guns, and then—you have the opportunity of winning the victories of peace—"

"Of which the world seldom hears," interpolated the Prince.

"But that makes it finer," she said. "Have we any real diplomats, who—oh, I don't know—make themselves felt in the inner circle of things: men that we—that the country—does not know of, who are doing the—the things you are?"

The Prince smiled.

"I don't know really. You have the 'new diplomacy' which is shouting what other people whisper—or keep to themselves—and *le gros gourdin*—the laughable big stick; it amuses us more than it impresses, I assure you." He regarded the girl closely and she smiled questioningly.

"You do not flush! You are not irritated?" he asked.

"Why should I be? What do you mean?"

"I was speaking lightly of your country."

"Oh, were you? I did not notice. I fear I am used to that, having spent much time in Europe."

The Prince looked at her curiously. She colored.

"No," she said, "I do not go in strongly for the *furore Americanus*, if that is what you mean."

"So. Your country must look to its *bourgeoise* for its Joans of Arc. But then your men are ungallantly self-sufficient. In Russia," the Prince shrugged his shoulders, "we send women to Siberia—or decorate them with the Order of St. Katherine."

"You actually shame me, Prince Koltsoff. We are different here; even our suffragettes would by no means allow devotion to their cause to carry them to jail; and as for influencing statesmen, or setting their plans at naught—" she shook her head—"why, I do not even know who they are. They are not in our set," laughing. "Really, we are pretty much butterflies from your—from any—viewpoint, are n't we? But after all, why?"

"Ah, why?" He turned to her suddenly. "Do you love your country, Miss Wellington?"

"What an absurd question! Of course I do."

"Easily answered," replied the Prince, "but think a moment. I said *love*. That love which inspired your women to send their sons and husbands to die for their country in your Civil War; the love that exalted Charlotte Corday. Have you breathed the quicker when you saw your flag in foreign lands?" He looked at her strangely. "Would you loathe the man you loved if you learnt he had injured your country? Think, Miss Wellington."

"Your fervor renders it quite impossible for me to think; if it will satisfy you I will say I don't believe I begin to know what patriotism is. Yet I would not have you think I am altogether shallow. Sir Clarence Pembroke has praised my grasp of British affairs. I have always regarded that as quite a compliment."

"You have reason. You know, we know, that the American woman who would move in the tense affairs of the world must find her opportunity in Europe. It does not exist here."

"And never can exist, in a republic, I imagine," said the girl, "at least in a republic constituted as ours is."

"No, surely not. By-the-bye, who is your Secretary of the Navy? Your Attorney-General?"

"Help!" cried the girl in mock despair. "Really, Prince Koltsoff, I must ask you to consider your demonstration of my unfitness to even consider myself an American complete. Further humiliation is unnecessary. At least I suppose I should feel humiliated. But somehow, I 'm not. That's the pitiable part of it."

"And yet, Miss Wellington, have you ever considered what would lie before you with your,—pardon me,—your beauty and your wit, in Europe?"

"No, I never have," said Anne not quite truthfully. "Please, Prince Koltsoff, let us change the subject."

CHAPTER VIII
WHEN A PRINCE WOOS

But Prince Koltsoff evidently deemed it expedient to obey the letter, not the spirit, of the wish. An ardent lover of horses, he gave himself wholly to them when they arrived at the stables, conversing freely with the grooms and going over the various equines with the hands and eyes of an expert.

When at length they strolled from the stables to a little wooded knoll near the boundary of the estate, commanding a view of the main road, which ran straight for a quarter of a mile and then dived into the purple hills with their gray out-jutting rocks, the girl, who had been left pretty much to her own thoughts, felt in ever-growing degree the disadvantage at which she had been placed in the course of their conversation. She had sat, it seemed, as a child at the feet of a tutor. At least in the mood she had developed, she would have it so. The thought did not please her. And then she began to burn with the memory that on the veranda the Prince had placed his hand upon hers and that for some reason beyond her knowledge, she had permitted it to remain so until he had withdrawn it.

This sufferance, she felt, had somehow affected, at the very outset, a degree of tacit intimacy between them which would not otherwise have occurred in a fortnight, perhaps never. But he had done it with an assurance almost, if not quite, hypnotic, and he had removed his hand—a move, she recognized, which offered more opportunities for bungling than the initial venture—with the exact degree of insouciance, of abstraction, but at the same time not without a slight lighting of the eyes expressive alike of humility and gratitude. Lurking in her mind was an irritation over the position in which she had been placed, and her only solace was the thought that her revenge might be taken when Koltsoff tried it again, as she had no doubt he would.

If she had analyzed her emotions she would have been obliged to face the disagreeable truth that she, Anne Wellington, was jealous. Jealous of a stable of horses! After all, introspection, however deep, might not have opened her eyes as to the basic element of her mood, for jealousy had never been among the components of her mental equipment. At all events she was, as she would have expressed it, "peeved." Why? Because he had held her hand—and talked to her like a school girl.

But silence, smilingly indifferent, was the only manifestation of her state of mind. If he noticed this he said nothing to indicate that he did, but resumed his conversation as though no interruption had occurred. And curiously enough even her simulation of indifference disappeared as he turned to her, bringing words and all the subtle charm of his personality to bear. Strange elation possessed him and she yielded again as freely as before to that indescribable air of the world which characterized his every action and word. He spoke English with but the faintest accent. Once he lapsed into French, speaking as rapidly as a native. Anne caught him perfectly and answered him at some length in the same tongue. Koltsoff stopped short and gazed at her glowingly.

"There, you have demonstrated what I have been trying to say so poorly. Permit me to carry on my point more intimately. Yes, it is so; you are typically an American girl. But wherein do such young women, such as you, my dear Miss Wellington, find their *métier*? In America? In New York? In Newport? No. They are abroad; the wives of diplomats, cabinet ministers, or royal councillors of France, Germany, Austria, Italy, and," the Prince bowed slightly, "of my native land. Here, what lies before you? Ah," he stooped and snatched a bit of clover, "I have seen, I have studied, have I not? Washington, what is it to you? A distant place. And its affairs? Bah, merely items to be skipped in the newspapers. As you have admitted, you know nothing of them. You do not know your cabinet officers; and so you marry and—and what do you Americans say?—settle down."

"How knowingly you picture us," smiled the girl.

The Prince waved his hands.

"You travel, yes, but at best, most significantly, your lives are narrow. You are wives and mothers, living in ruts as well-defined as those of your most prosaic middle-class women. What do you know of the inner world, its moving affairs? Who of you can read the significance, open though it may be, of the cabled statement or speech of a prime minister, in relation to America?"

"Perhaps our opportunities or incentives do not exist," replied the girl gravely. "I have heard father say ours is a government of politicians and not statesmen."

"Precisely, that is it. But in Europe, where conditions are different, what do we find? Lady Campbell in Egypt—an American girl; the Princess Stein in St. Petersburg; the Marquise de Villiers in France; Lady Clanclaren in London—oh, scores, all American girls, some of whom have made their influence felt constructively, as I can personally assure you. American history is so uninteresting because there is not a woman in it."

"You know the Marquise de Villiers!" exclaimed the girl. "Won't you tell me, sometime, all about her? How interesting her story must be! I have heard garbled versions of the Berlin incident."

"I do know her," the Prince smiled, as he thought how intimate his knowledge was, "and I shall delight in telling you all about her sometime. But now," he continued, "allow me to carry on my thought. You travel—yes. You even live abroad as the, ah, butterfly—your own word—lives. I know. Have not I heard of you! Have I not followed you in the newspapers since I saw your face on canvas! I read from a *dossier* that I formulated concerning you." He drew a notebook from his pocket and glanced at the girl. "May I?"

"It is yours," was the reply.

"January," he read, "Miss W. is tobogganing in Switzerland. February, she is viewing the Battle of Flowers at Nice. March, she is at Monaco, at Monte Carlo—ah! April, Miss W. has arrived in Paris. May and June, she is in London. July, she is attending English race meetings with young Clanclaren—" the Prince paused with a sibilant expulsion of breath. "I must not read my comment."

"Yes, you must, please. I never heard of such a romantic Russian!"

The Prince raised his eyebrows and glanced at the book—"with young Clanclaren, damn him! August," continued Koltsoff hurriedly, drowning her subdued exclamation, "at Clanclaren's Scotch shooting box. September, she is again in England, deer stalking—most favored deer! October, November, she is riding to hounds in England. December, she is doing the grand tour of English country houses." The Prince paused. "So, our acquaintance—my acquaintance with you—is of more than a few days. I have known you for more than a year. Do you find it not agreeable?"

"Not agreeable! I don't know. I am—I—I—oh, I don't know, it seems almost uncanny to me."

"Not at all, my dear Miss Wellington. Surely not uncanny. Let us ascribe it to the genius of Sargent; to the inspiration of a face on canvas."

"But you really haven't known me at all. You—"

He interrupted.

"Know you! Ah, don't I! I know you above these trivial things. The world of affairs will feel the impress of your personality, of your wit, your intellect—of your beauty. Then vale the idle, flashing days of pleasure. Iron will enter into your life. But you will rejoice. For who is there that finds power not joyous? Ambassadors will confide in you. Prime ministers will forget the interests of their offices." He paused. "Who knows when or how soon? But it shall be, surely, inevitably.... I wonder," he was speaking very slowly now, "if you will recognize your opportunity."

"Who knows," she said softly. The Prince remained silent, looking at her. She seemed to feel the necessity of further words but was wholly without inspiration. She glanced down the road and saw a boy in blue toiling along on a bicycle. Her exclamation was out of all proportion to the event.

"A messenger boy! He brings word from father—we expect him to-morrow, you know."

"He brings no word from your father," replied the Prince mysteriously. "His errand concerns me. You shall see." They moved to the gate and the boy alighting, glanced at the two with his alert Irish eyes.

"Say, does a fellow named Koltsoff live here?"

"I am he; give me the package, boy. It is prepaid—very well; here is something for you," tossing the urchin a quarter.

"Thanks," said the boy, who suddenly paused in the act of remounting his wheel and clapped his hand to his pocket. "Here's a letter, too."

As he rode away the two slowly retraced their steps.

"You will pardon me if I read this note?"

Anne, strangely abstracted, nodded, and Koltsoff tore open the envelope. As he read the letter his brow darkened.

"Gone!" he muttered. Then he read the letter again.

Yeasky would not have departed without the best of reasons. He held the inked-out line to the light but could make nothing of it. He walked along beside the girl in deep thought. His hands trembled. He knew that in his possession was that which represented the triumph of his career. There were few honors which a grateful Government would withhold from him. Besides, it meant the probable rehabilitation of the prestige of the Russian arms; that thought thrilled him no less, for he was a patriot.

And yet amid all his exaltation indecision filled him. Duty pointed a direct and immediate course to St. Petersburg. Other emotions dictated his remaining at The Crags. The package could not be intrusted to the express companies. It must be carried personally to Russia. And yet—and yet he could not leave Newport now. Just a little while! He must wait. To his Czar, to his country, he owed haste; to himself he owed delay. Which debt should he cancel? Suddenly with a sharp upward turn of the head he dismissed all conflicting thoughts from his mind, refused utterly to allow them to remain, and turned to the girl. They were entering a small grove of trees.

An inspiration had flashed over him, dominant, compelling. He spoke impulsively, almost wildly; so much so that Anne stopped, startled. In his outstretched hand the package was within a few inches of her face.

"Miss Wellington," he cried, "we were speaking of opportunities, but a while ago. May I call upon you now? I have said I am not in Newport for pleasure alone. A great matter has been consummated. I hold it in my hand. Who can trust servants? My valet? No! Who? Can I trust you, Miss Wellington? Can I place my honor, my life, in your hands, for a week, not more?"

"Why, I—" began Anne.

"Is it then too much to ask?"

"I hope not, Prince Koltsoff. Tell me and then I can judge."

"So!" and Koltsoff held out the package to her. "Keep this for me. Let no one know where it is except myself. Keep it until I ask for it. If matters arise of such nature to prevent my asking, keep it still. Keep it!" Koltsoff was now acting as he loved to act. "Keep it until I ask for it; or until I am dead. If the latter, throw it over the cliffs. My country is on the verge of a war with—with you may guess whom. Japan, no less. That, that which you hold in your hand is the heart of our hopes." He paused.

He was really sincere. His desire was to forestall any defeat of his plans by having the package out of his hands until such time as he would leave Newport. One of his valets had once been successfully bribed. But equally did he desire that the girl should have a bond of interest akin to his; through this, he knew, must lie the success of that understanding which alone kept him from following Yeasky out of Newport forthwith.

But the girl could not know this. Her pride in sharing in so intimate a way a matter which she believed to—and for that matter, really did—affect the policy of a great empire, held her spellbound. There was the feminine delight, too, in being on the inner side of a mystery.

She nodded mechanically. "I shall do as you ask," she said.

The Prince sprang forward, caught her hands and pressed upon them hot, lingering kisses.

"Into these hands," he said, "I commit my destiny and my honor."

CHAPTER IX
ARMITAGE CHANGES HIS VOCATION

Half an hour after the incident at Trinity, Armitage hurried from the little ferry boat which had just landed him at the Torpedo Station and made his way to the house of the storekeeper, who was out, of course. He had gone to Providence, his wife said, and would return about four o'clock.

Armitage took the key to the shops, only to find when he entered that the storekeeper's books were in the safe, the combination to which he did not know. This by no means improved his temper and he began to blunder about the office in a dragnet search. Finally, when he found himself kicking over chairs which were in his way in his aimless course, the humor of the situation came to him. He sat down upon a tool chest and laughed aloud.

Clearly, there was nothing for him to do in the absence of Jackson—except go to his dinner; which he did. A few minutes before three o'clock, he went to the office again and sat down to wait for Yeasky. He gave the man half an hour overtime and then nodded grimly and dismissed any lingering notion he might have entertained concerning his honesty.

When the storekeeper appeared some time later, Armitage was still at his desk idly drawing diagrams on a pad.

"Mr. Jackson," he said, "I hate to bother you to-day, but things have happened which seem to make it necessary to check those parts now—" Armitage arose briskly.

The storekeeper waved his hands.

"Oh, I checked them up this morning," he said.

"Everything straight?" snapped Armitage.

"Why—yes," Jackson fumbled in his desk. "Here is the sheet."

Armitage seized it and glanced up and down the various items.

"Bully work, Mr. Jackson!" He looked up with a sigh of relief. "Everything seems correct. George! That takes a load off my mind. Let's see." He went down the list with his finger. "I understand you, don't I?" he said, handing the sheet to the storekeeper.

"Understand?"

"I mean, this is a list taken from the tally sheet of parts, all of which you have found to be in the office? In other words," he added rapidly, "everything that appears on this sheet is now, at the present time, inside this office?"

"Yes—everything, except—" the storekeeper paused an instant, looking at Armitage with sudden doubt.

"Except what?" cried the officer impatiently.

"Why, that special core of the magnetic control. You have that, haven't you? It is n't in the shop."

"Is n't in the shop! Well, where the devil is it then?"

"Why," exclaimed the storekeeper, "no one ever handled that but you. Not even Yeasky. You never let any one even see it. I remember how careful you have been about that."

"I know," Armitage rose from his chair. "But it was never out of the shop. It was always in the big safe. Have you looked there?" He turned to Jackson hopefully.

But the storekeeper shook his head.

"Are you sure you have looked everywhere?"

"It is not in the shop—I thought sure you must have it. Does it—was it vitally important?"

"Important!" Armitage threw himself into a chair and put his feet on the desk. "Well, Jackson, I fancy you might call it so. Damn!"

The storekeeper whistled.

"I shall have the rooms of the workmen searched."

"Just one room, please; and quickly, will you?" rejoined Armitage, "Yeasky's. He is the only man who would have known its value. Give my compliments to the superintendent and ask him for some one to help you."

As the storekeeper departed, Joe Thornton entered the office.

"Any luck, Jack?"

"Rotten! The magnetic control of the model is gone. I was right this morning and you were wrong, Joe. Yeasky got it. Why did n't I keep my hands on him, when I had him! Something told me to."

"The deuce!" Thornton regarded his friend with a grave face. "Is it very serious? Does it give the whole snap away?"

"It gives about ninety per cent more away than pleases me. It would take some genius long nights of labor to supply the other ten per cent even with the aid of the plans which no doubt Yeasky has copied. That is, there are one or two things that I kept off the paper—kept in my head." He paced up and down the floor. "But other men have heads, too. That thing has got to be returned, the quicker the better."

"Well," Thornton smiled encouragingly. "Yeasky can't get out of the country—and he'll be caught before he dopes the thing out. Even if he has mailed or expressed it, it can be held up before it leaves this country. You had the control in the model torpedo last night. Have you wired?"

"I've sent a general call to the secret service for him, to Boston, New York, and Washington. They are holding the telegrams, as long as letters, at the telegraph office for release. I've also a wire to the Department on file, telling what has happened. I wrote before I knew what was gone, so I would n't have to lie in case he took what he did take."

"Yes," agreed Thornton, "there is no use in letting on how bad it really is."

Thornton was growing quite optimistic.

"Yeasky can't get away; you'll have the thing back here within three days."

Armitage smiled.

"Not through capturing Yeasky. He hasn't it now. You don't suppose he is enough of a fool to risk being caught with the goods, do you? He got that thing off his hands, quick."

"Transferred it! Who to?"

Armitage shrugged his shoulders.

"To Prince Koltsoff."

"Koltsoff! How do you know?"

"How do I know anything that isn't as plain as a pikestaff? Common sense! Prince Koltsoff has that thing right now." Armitage grinned. "The noble guest of the house of Ronald Wellington playing the spy—and rather successfully. Quite an interesting society item, eh?"

Thornton did not smile.

"Look here, old man, what is your drift? Prince Koltsoff! Old boy, this is serious! It is nothing to smile about. Say, do you know what this means?"

"Oh, no!" said Armitage sarcastically. "Oh, I don't mean the loss to yourself and the Government, I mean the politics of it. Jack, every nation knows about that torpedo. You know the *attachés* that have been snooping round here on one pretence or another since you have been working. Japan knows about it; you know her situation with Russia. Russia gets your torpedo—what's Japan going to do? What will England say? How can the Government prove it was stolen? Oh, we can say so but we 'd say so anyway, would n't we? How will you look?" Thornton threw up his hands and confronted Armitage. "I tell you, Jack, it's a nasty mess. Your status in the matter will size up about like a pin point at Washington. You 've got to catch Yeasky, somehow."

"Fine, bright boy!" Armitage twisted a newspaper in his hands, broke it, and tossed the two ends away. "I don't want Yeasky, I tell you. You 're off the track. I want Koltsoff. The secret service fellows can go after Yeasky. It's perfectly certain he turned that control over to Koltsoff, after, if not before, I held him up. He knew he was suspected. Anyway, the Russian was undoubtedly here to receive it. Why else would he be here?"

"Anne Wellington, so the *Saunterer* says."

Armitage turned quickly upon his friend and brother officer.

"Anne, nothing!" he fairly snarled. "I remember about Koltsoff now. Worcester was once *attaché* at St. Petersburg and told me all about him last summer. He 's just a plain, ordinary, piking crook. But he 's up against the wrong kind of diplomacy this time. I 'll get him before he leaves Newport and choke that magnetic control out of him. Come over to the *D'Estang* a minute, Joe; I want to show you something.... Well, Mr. Jackson, cleaned out? I thought so. Thank you, I am going to be away for a few days. Don't let anything be touched, please. Let the work stop until I return. Come on, Joe."

In his cabin on the *D'Estang*, Armitage pointed to several more or less disreputable garments lying on his berth.

"Say," he said, "would a candidate for physical instructor for the Wellington boys wear such clothes?"

Thornton looked hard at his friend for a minute and then his face broadened into a huge smile of understanding. "Not if he wanted the job," he said. "You 'll make more of a hit as you are."

"All right, and now, Joe, go into the yeoman's office like a good chap, pick out a time-stained sheet of paper and typewrite a letter, signing your name as captain of the 19— football eleven at Annapolis, saying that the bearer, Jack—Jack—who?"

"McCall," suggested Thornton.

"Yes, McCall—saying that Jack McCall had given great satisfaction as trainer for the eleven and was honest and God-fearing; you know how to do it."

"All right," said Thornton, starting for the door. He paused in the corridor. "Say, Jack, do you know you're taking all this mighty light?" He frowned. "This is serious."

Armitage frowned too.

"I know, but I 'll be serious enough before it's over, I reckon."

"You will," said Thornton dryly. "How do you expect to get the job anyway?"

Armitage shrugged his shoulders.

"Leave that to me," he said. "Oh, Joe, are you going to be on the island for supper?"

"No—not for supper," he said. "I 'll be over from Newport about eleven o'clock though."

"All right, drop aboard then, will you? I want to see you."

"Right-o," said Thornton.

For some time after his departure Armitage sat writing a document, covering the case to date, outlining his plans, his suspicions and the like. It turned out to be lengthy. He sealed it in an envelope, labelled it, "Armitage vs. Koltsoff," and locked it in a small safe in the yeoman's room.

One of the engineer's force came in to say that they had made progress in repairing the boiler baffle plates, designed to keep the funnels from torching when under high speed, but that they were at the point where advice was needed.

Armitage arose, put on a suit of greasy overalls, and went into the grimy vitals of the destroyer, a wrench in one hand, a chisel in the other. In about ten minutes he had solved the problem, explained it to the mechanics gathered about him, and then demonstrated just how simple the remedial measures were. All torpedo boat officers do this more often than not. It explains the blind fidelity with which the crews of craft of this sort accompany their officers without a murmur under the bows of swiftly moving battleships or through crowded ocean lanes at night without lights, with life boats aboard having aggregate capacity for about half the crew.

Armitage was alone at supper, his junior taking tea aboard a German cruiser in the harbor. With the coffee he lighted a cigar and half closed his eyes. He marvelled at the strange thrill which had possessed him since

Thornton had gone. The loss of that control was something which justified the gravest fears and deepest gloom. And yet—and yet—whenever he thought about it he saw, not Yeasky, nor Koltsoff, nor the torpedo—just a tall, flexible girl, with wonderful hair and eyes and lips. He puffed impatiently at his cigar. Hang it all, he had gone to church that morning because he felt he had to see her, and the morrow had been a blank because he knew he should not be able to see her again. But now, well, it looked as though he should see her; swift blood tingled in his cheeks.

Precisely at eleven Thornton looked in. Armitage gave him the combination of the safe, told him about the letter, and explained how he expected to obtain employment. They parted at midnight.

"Good-night, Jack," said Thornton, placing his hand affectionately on his brother officer's shoulder. "Now don't forget to dodge the interference and tackle low. And if you want me, 'phone. Consider me a minute man until you return."

"Thanks," replied Armitage. "Oh, Joe, will you mail this letter to the Department?" His voice lowered as he added half humorously, "It seems almost a shame to set the dogs on a man who may prove to be a benefactor."

"What?" asked Thornton.

"Nothing; good-night, Joe."

CHAPTER X
JACK MCCALL, AT YOUR SERVICE

Armitage landed in Newport by the eight o'clock boat and calling a hack drove out to the house of the chief of police. The chief was at breakfast and came to the door with his napkin in his hand. He greeted his visitor with a broad smile of welcome.

"Hello, Lieutenant," he said. "What's doing? Another of your boys you want turned loose?"

"Good-morning, Chief. No, not exactly. May I talk to you a minute?"

"Sure." The chief glanced about the dining room and closed the door with his foot. "Talk as much as you like."

Armitage glanced at the chief with an admiring smile. He had never ceased to wonder at the multifarious qualities which enabled the man to remain indispensable to native and cottager alike. Courteous, handsome, urbane, diplomatic, debonair, when a matron of the very highest caste sent for him to enlist his efforts in the regaining of some jewel, tiara, or piece of *vertu*, missing after a weekend, he never for a moment forgot that it was all a bit of carelessness, which the gentlest sort of reminder would correct. This is to say that he usually brought about the return of the missing article and neither of the parties between which he served as intermediary ever felt the slightest embarrassment or annoyance. No wedding was ever given without consulting him as to the proper means to be employed in guarding the presents. He was at once a social register, containing the most minute and extensive data, and an *index criminis*, unabridged.

As Armitage talked, the chief's eyes lighted and he nodded his head approvingly from time to time.

"I see," he said. "It's rather clever of you. I'll hold myself for any word. I can do more: I know Mrs. Wellington quite well. You can ask her to call me for reference if you wish. I'll make you out a fine thug."

"That'll be fine, although I may not need you. In the meantime have your men keep an eye out for Yeasky. And," Armitage paused, "if Koltsoff—never mind; we've first to prove our case."

"Yes, that would be about the wisest thing you could do," observed the chief. "Good luck."

An hour later Armitage stood in the servants' sitting-room confronting Miss Hatch, Mrs. Wellington's secretary, who was viewing him, not without interest.

"Mrs. Wellington will see you, I think," she said. "She usually breakfasts early and should be in her office now."

Armitage had an engaging grin which invariably brought answering smiles even from the veriest strangers. So now the crisp, bespectacled young woman was smiling broadly when Armitage shrugged his shoulders.

"Mrs. Wellington?" he said. "I had an idea I should have to see Mr. Wellington."

"By no means," asserted the secretary. "Wait a moment, please."

In a few minutes the young woman returned and nodded.

"Will you come with me, please?"

She led the way up a winding pair of stairs and down a long hall with heavy crimson carpet, turning into a room near the rear of the house. Mrs. Wellington was at her desk looking over a menu which the housekeeper had just submitted. She glanced up as the two entered, her face unchanging in expression.

"This is Mr. McCall," said the secretary, who without further words went to her desk and unlimbered the typewriter.

As Mrs. Wellington brought Armitage under her scrutiny, which was long, silent, and searching, he felt as he did upon his first interview with the Secretary of the Navy. However, no one had ever accused him of lack of nerve.

"You apply for the position of physical instructor to my sons," she said at length. "How did you know we wanted one?"

Armitage, caught for the instant off his guard, stammered.

"I—at least Miss—I mean I read it in one of the papers."

"Hum," replied Mrs. Wellington, "a rather misleading medium. Correct in this instance, though."

"I believe it was an advertisement," said Armitage.

"What qualifications have you?"

Armitage smiled easily.

"I have taught boxing, wrestling, and jiu-jitsu in Southern athletic clubs," he said, "and I trained the 19— navy team at Annapolis."

He submitted Thornton's eloquent testimonial. Mrs. Wellington laid it aside after a glance.

"Where is your home?"

"Louisville, Kentucky, ma'm."

"What have you been doing in Newport? I remember having seen you at church yesterday morning."

"I came up to see Winthrop of the Harvard Graduate Advisory Committee on Athletics about getting the job as trainer for the football team next month. He is away."

"Were you ever in college?" asked Mrs. Wellington.

Armitage assumed a look of embarrassment.

"Yes," he said, "but unless you insist I had rather not say where or why I left."

Mrs. Wellington sniffed.

"I thought so," she observed drily. "What would you do for my sons?"

Armitage was on his favorite topic now.

"I 'd try to convince them that it pays to be strong and clean in mind and body—" he began earnestly, when a rustle of skirts and the click of footsteps at the threshold caused him to turn. Anne Wellington, in an embroidered white linen frock, stood framed in the doorway, smiling at them.

"Pardon me, mother," she said, "but I am in a dreadful fix." She glanced toward Armitage. "This is our new physical instructor, is it not?"

"He has applied for the position," said Mrs. Wellington, not altogether blithely.

"How fortunate—" began the girl and then stopped abruptly. "That is," she added, "if he can drive a car."

"I helped make automobiles in Chicago," Armitage ventured.

"Good!" exclaimed Anne. "You know, mother, Rimini has gone to New York to receive that Tancredi, and Benoir, the second chauffeur, is in the hospital. I must have a driver for a day or so. He may for a while, may he not, mother?" She nodded to Armitage. "If you will go out to the garage, please, I shall have Mr. Dawson give you some clothing. I think he can fit you. I—"

"One moment, Anne," interrupted her mother. "You do run on so. Just wait one moment. You seem to forget I am, or at least was, about to engage McCall as a physical instructor, not a *mécanicien*." Mrs. Wellington was fundamentally opposed to being manoeuvred, and her daughter's apparent attempt at *finesse* in this matter irritated her. She was fully bent now upon declining to employ Armitage in any capacity and was on the point of saying so, when Anne, who had diagnosed her trend of mind, broke in.

"Really, mother, I am perfectly sincere. But this situation, you must admit, was totally unexpected—and I must have a driver, don't you know. Why, I 've planned to take Prince Koltsoff, oh, everywhere."

This won for her. Mrs. Wellington even when irritated was altogether capable of viewing all sides of a matter.

"Very well," she said. "I shall consider the other matter. When you are through with McCall, let me know."

Anne's eyes sparkled with relief.

"Mother, you are a dear." She walked over and touched her affectionately on her arm. "McCall, if you will go out to the garage, Mr. Dawson will show you your room and give you some clothes. I may want you any time, so please don't go far from the garage."

As Armitage passed out, guided by Miss Hatch, Mrs. Wellington turned to her daughter.

"Well, Anne," she said, "he lied and lied and lied. But I do believe some of the things he said and some he did n't. I believe him to be honest and I believe he will be good for the boys. He himself is a magnificent specimen, certainly. But I don't reconcile one thing."

"What is that, mother?"

"He is a gentleman and has been bred as one; that is perfectly evident."

"Oh, no doubt," replied her daughter with apparent indifference. "One of the younger son variety you meet in and out of England, I fancy."

"I suppose so," said Mrs. Wellington. "Is that why you invited him to sit with us in church? Why you spoke to him on the *General*? Why you wanted me to employ him?"

"I don't know," replied Anne frankly. "He interested me. He does yet. He is a mystery and I want to solve him."

"May an old woman give you a bit of advice, Anne? Thank you," as her daughter bowed. "Remember he is an employee of this house. He sought the position; he must be down to it. Keep that in your mind—and don't let him drive fast. In the meantime, how about his license?"

Anne stamped her foot.

"Oh, dear!" she exclaimed. "I forgot all about that beastly license. What can we do?" She faced her mother. "Mother, can't you think of something? I know you can arrange it if you will."

"Well," said her mother thoughtfully. Suddenly she looked at her secretary who entered at the moment. "Miss Hatch, you might get Chief Roberts on the 'phone—right away, please. Now, Anne, I am getting nervous; you had better go."

"Yes, mother." Anne dropped a playful curtsey and left the room, smiling.

Half an hour later, Armitage, squeezed into a beautifully made suit of tan whipcord, his calves swathed in putees, and a little cap with vizor pressing flat against his brows, was loitering about the garage with Ryan, a footman, and absorbing the gossip of the family. Prince Koltsoff was still there and intended, evidently, to remain for some time. This information, gained from what Anne Wellington had said to her mother, had relieved his mind of fears that his quarry had already gone, and he would have been quite at his ease had not the thought that the fact of Koltsoff's presence here rather argued against his having the control in his possession, occurred to him. Still, if the Russian had any of the instincts of a gentleman he could hardly break away from the Wellingtons at such short notice, and certainly not if he was, as Thornton surmised, interested in the daughter. Talk about the garage left him in no doubt of this.

If the Prince had the missing part he would do one of three things: hold onto it until he left; mail it; or express it to St. Petersburg. Benoir, he had learned, carried the Wellington mail as well as express matter to the city, mornings and afternoons. In his absence, Armitage was, he felt, the logical man for this duty. So he did not worry about these contingencies. He had knowledge that up to eight o'clock that morning no package for foreign countries had been either mailed or expressed; this eliminated the fear, which might otherwise have been warrantable, that the package had already been sent on its way to Europe. Besides, no man of Koltsoff's experience would be likely to trust the delivery of so important an object to any but his own hands. Thus the probabilities were that the thing was at this minute in the Prince's room. If all these suppositions were wrong, then Yeasky had it. Armitage knew enough of the workings of the Secret Service Bureau to know that if the man got out of the country he would be an elusive person indeed, especially as he had a long, livid scar across his left cheek which could not be concealed with any natural effect.

But, somehow, the conviction persisted in Armitage's mind that the Prince had the control. In the short time he had spent at The Crags this impression had not diminished; it had increased, without definite reason, to be sure; and yet, the fact remained. He would find out one way or another shortly. His room, not in the servants' wing, was on the third floor, right over the apartments of the Wellington boys, which in turn were not far from Koltsoff's suite. It would not be long before a burglary would be committed in the Wellington house. At this thought, Armitage thrilled with delightful emotions.

In the meantime he addressed himself to the task of gleaning further information concerning the family into whose employ he had entered. He learned that while Mr. Wellington and his daughter were devoted to motoring, Mrs. Wellington would have none of it, and that the boys were inclined to horses also. Ronald Wellington left things pretty much to his wife and she was a "Hellian," as Ryan put it, to those about her who were not efficient and faithful. But otherwise, she was a pretty decent sort and willing to pay well.

"What sort are the boys?" asked Armitage, recalling that his duties with them might begin at any time.

"Master Ronald, the oldest, is stuck on himself," replied Ryan. "He ain't easy to get along with. Master Royal, the youngster, is as fine a little chap as ever lived. Ronald is learning himself the cigarette habit; which is all right— the quicker he smokes himself to death the better, if he was n't after learnin' young Muck, as every one calls him, to smoke, too. They do it on the quiet here in the garage, although it's against the rules."

"Why don't you stop them then?" asked Armitage.

Ryan shrugged and laughed.

"If we stopped them we 'd be fired for committin' insult and if they 're caught here we 'll be fired for lettin' 'em smoke. That's the way with those who work for people like the Wellingtons—always between the devil and the deep sea."

"Oh, I don't know," said Armitage, whose combative instincts were now somewhat aroused, "I don't think people get into great trouble for doing their duty, whoever they work for."

The footman grinned.

"Well," he said, "you 'll know more about that the longer you 're here."

As he spoke, the boys under discussion entered the doorway and seating themselves upon the running board of a touring car, helped themselves to cigarettes from a silver case which the elder took from his pocket. They lighted them without a glance at the two men and had soon filled the atmosphere with pungent smoke.

"Do they do this often?" asked Armitage at length, turning to Ryan and speaking in a voice not intended to be hidden.

The footman grinned and nodded.

"Against the rules, isn't it?" persisted Armitage, much to Ryan's evident embarrassment, who, however, nodded again.

The older boy took his cigarette from his mouth and rising, walked a few steps toward the new chauffeur. He was a slender stripling with high forehead, long, straight nose, and a face chiefly marked by an imperious expression. In his flannels and flapping Panama hat he was a reduced copy of such Englishmen as Armitage had seen lounging in the boxes at Ascot or about the paddock at Auteuil.

"Were you speaking of us, my man?" he said.

A gleam of amusement crossed Armitage's face.

"I—I believe I was, my boy. Why?"

A corner of the youth's upper lip curled and snapping the half-burnt cigarette into a corner he took another from the case and lighted it.

"Oh," he said nodding, "you are the new man. Impertinence is not a good beginning. I 'm afraid you won't last."

Armitage crossed quickly to the discarded cigarette which was smouldering near a little pool of gasoline under a large can of that dangerous fluid, and rubbed the fire out with his foot. Returning, he confronted the boy, standing very close to him.

"Look here, son," he said quietly, "that won't do a bit, you know. It's against the rules, and besides," jerking his head in the direction of the gasoline can, "you have n't any sense."

Ronald's emotions were beyond the power of words to relieve. As he stood glaring at Armitage, his face devoid of color, his eyes green with anger, the chauffeur placed his hand gently upon his arm.

"You can't smoke here, I tell you. There 's a notice over there to that effect signed by your father. Now throw that cigarette away; or go out of here with it, as you like."

By way of reply, Ronald jerked his arm from Armitage's grasp and swung at his face with open hand. It was a venomous slap, but it did not come within a foot of the mark for the reason that Jack deftly caught the flailing arm by the wrist and with a powerful twist brought young Wellington almost to his knees through sheer pain of the straining tendons. As this happened, the younger brother with a shrill cry of rage launched himself at Armitage, who caught him by the waist and swung him easily up into the tonneau of the touring car.

Ronald had risen to his feet and in cold passion was casting his eye about the garage. A heavy wrench lay on the floor; he stepped towards it, but not too quickly for Armitage to interpose. Slowly the latter raised his finger until it was on a level with the boy's face.

"Now, stop just a minute and think," he said. "I like your spirit, and yours, too, kid," he added, gazing up at the tonneau from which the younger Wellington was glaring down like a bellicose young tiger, "but this won't go at all. Now wait," as Ronald tried to brush past. "In the first place, if your mother hears you have been smoking in the garage—or anywhere else—you'll get into trouble with her, so Ryan has told me. And I don't believe that's any fun.... Now—listen, will you? I am employed here as physical instructor for you chaps, not as a chauffeur—although your sister has been good enough to press me into service for a day or two—and I imagine I'm going to draw pay for making you into something else than thin-chested cigarette fiends. I can do it, if you'll help. How about it?" he said, smiling at Ronald. "Will you be friends?"

Ronald, who had worked out of his passion, sniffed.

"Thank you, I had rather not, if you don't mind. I think you will find that you don't like your place."

"Well," said Armitage affably, "then I can leave, you know."

"Yes, you can, all right; it'll be sooner than you think. Come on, Muck," and the older brother turned and left the garage.

Muck, who for the past few seconds had been gazing at Armitage with wide eyes, slipped down from the car and stood in front of him.

"Say," he exclaimed, "you're the fellow I gave that note to in church—the one from my sister—are n't you?"

He grinned as Armitage looked at him dumbly.

"Don't be afraid," he said. "I shan't tell. Sister gave me a five-dollar gold piece. I thought you did n't act like a chauffeur. Say, show me that grip you got on Ronie, will you? He has been too fresh lately,—I want to spring it on him. Can I learn it?"

"Not that one." Armitage took the boy's hand, his thumb pressing back of the second knuckle, his fingers on the palm. He twisted backward and upward gently. "There 's one that's better, though, and easier. See? Not that way," as the boy seized his hand. "Press here. That's right. Now you 've got it. You can make your brother eat out of your hand."

"Thanks!" Muck left beaming, searching for his disgruntled brother—and Armitage had made a friend.

A minute later Royal, or Muck, as his nickname seemed to be, thrust his head into the garage. "You 're not going to say anything to mother about the cigarettes, are you?"

"That's the best guess you ever made," smiled Armitage. "You and I 'll settle that, won't we?"

"Rather," replied the boy, who departed with a nod.

"Well, you 've done it," said Ryan, gazing at Armitage admiringly. "Master Ronald will raise hell!"

Armitage shook his head.

"I don't care, I just had to devil that rooster. He was insufferable. I—"

The telephone bell rang, and Ryan, with a significant I-told-you-so grimace took up the receiver. A second later a smile of relief lighted his face.

"Very well. Thank you, sir," he said, and turned to Armitage.

"The butler, Mr. Buchan, says that Miss Wellington would have you bring out her car at once. She don't want any footman."

Armitage arose with a thrill which set his ears tingling, cranked the motor, and within a minute was rolling out of the garage.

CHAPTER XI
THE DYING GLADIATOR

She was waiting, when Armitage, who was leaning back in his seat in the most professional manner, shut off power under the *porte cochère* and glanced at her for directions.

"To Mrs. Van Valkenberg's," she said. "Do you know where she lives?"

"No, I don't, Miss Wellington."

"No matter, I'll direct you."

As they entered the Ocean Drive through an archway of privet, Miss Wellington indicated a road which dived among the hills and disappeared.

"Drive quite slowly," she said.

It was a beautiful road, dipping and rising, but hidden at all times by hills, resplendent with black and yellow and purple gorse, or great gray bowlders, so that impressions of Scotch moorlands alternated with those of an Arizona desert. The tang of September was in the breeze; from the moorlands which overlooked the jagged Brenton reefs came the faint aroma of burning sedge; from the wet distant cliff a saline exhalation was wafted. It was such a morning as one can see and feel only on the island of Newport.

As an additional charm to Anne Wellington, there was the tone of time about it all. From childhood she had absorbed all these impressions of late Summer in Newport; they had grown, so to speak, into her life, had become a part of her nature. She drew a deep breath and leaned forward.

"Stop here a moment, will you please."

They were at the bottom of a hollow with no sign of habitation about, save the roof of a villa which perched upon a rocky eminence, half a mile to one side.

"Will you get out and lift the radiator cover and pretend to be fixing something, McCall? I want to talk to you."

Without a word, Jack left his seat, went to the tool box and was soon viewing the internal economy of the car, simulating search for an electrical hiatus with some fair degree of accuracy.

The girl bent forward, her cheek suffused but a humorous smile playing about her face.

"McCall," she said, "I feel I should assure you at the outset that I am quite aware of certain things."

Armitage glanced at her and then quickly lowered his eyes. She gazed admiringly at his strong, clean face and the figure sharply defined by the close-fitting livery.

"Your name is not McCall and I have not the slightest idea that you are by profession a physical instructor, or a driver either."

Armitage unscrewed a wrench and then screwed the jaws back into their place.

"We are what conditions make us, Miss Wellington," he said.

"Yes, that is true," she replied, "but tell me truthfully. Did you seek employment here only because of my—of my interest in—I mean, because of the note I wrote, or did you come because my note put you in the way of obtaining a needed position?"

Armitage started to speak and then stopped short. "Oh," he said finally, "I really needed the position."

The girl gazed at him a moment. Armitage, bending low, could see a patent leather pump protruding from the scalloped edge of her skirt, tapping the half-opened door of the tonneau.

"You will then pardon me," she said, "if I call to your mind the fact that you are now employed as driver of my car: I feel I have the right to ask you who you really are."

"Your mother—Mrs. Wellington, catechised me quite fully and I don't think I could add anything to what I told her."

"And what was that? I was not present during the inquisition," said the girl.

Armitage laughed.

"Why, I told her I was Jack McCall, that I came from Louisville, that I had trained the Navy eleven of 19—."

An exclamation from the girl interrupted him and he looked up. She was staring at him vacantly, as though ransacking the depths of memory.

"The Navy eleven of 19—," she said thoughtfully. Then she smiled. "McCall, you are so clever, really."

Armitage's eyes fell and he fumbled with the wrench.

"Thank you," he said, dubiously.

"Not at all, McCall," she said sweetly. "Listen," speaking rapidly, "I have always been crazy over football. Father was at Yale, '79, you know." She studied his face again, and then nodded. "When I was a girl, still in short dresses, father took a party of girls in Miss Ellis's school to Annapolis in his private car to see a Harvard-Navy game. A cousin of mine, Phil Disosway, was on the Harvard team. They were much heavier than Annapolis; but the score was very close, particularly because of the fine work of one of the Navy players who seemed to be in all parts of the field at once. I have forgotten his name,"—Miss Wellington gazed dreamily over the hills,— "but I can see him now, diving time after time into the interference and bringing down his man; catching punts and running—it was all such a hopeless fight, but such a brave, determined one." She shrugged her shoulders. "Really, I was quite carried away. As girls will, I—we, all of us— wove all sort of romantic theories concerning him. Toward the end of the game we could see him giving in under the strain and at last some coaches took him out. He walked tottering down the side lines past our stand, his face drawn and streaked with blood and dirt. I snapshotted that player. It was a good picture. I had it enlarged and have always kept it in my room. 'The Dying Gladiator,' I have called it. I wonder if you have any idea who that girlhood hero of mine was?"

"Was he a hero?" Armitage was bending over the carburetor. He waited a moment and then as Miss Wellington did not reply he added; "Now that you have placed me, I trust I shan't lose my position."

"I always knew I should see you again," said the girl as though she had not heard Armitage's banality. "I know now why I spoke to you on the *General* and why I wrote you that note in church." Her slipper beat an impatient tattoo on the door. "But why," she began, "why are you willing to enter service as a physical instructor, or motor car driver? I don't un—"

Armitage interrupted.

"Your mother asked me if I had been in college. I told her I had, but that I preferred not to say where, or why I left."

"Oh!" she said, and her eyes suffused with pity. "I am so sorry. But you *must* tell me one thing now. Was your leaving because of—of anything— that would make me sorry I had found—" she smiled, but looked at him eagerly—"the subject of the Dying Gladiator?"

"I hope not."

"You are not certain?"

"Miss Wellington, there are certain reasons why the position you helped me to obtain was vitally necessary. I am a dependant in your house. I can assure you that you will never find anything half so grievous against me as that which you have already found—your 'Dying Gladiator' a servant. You must think of that."

"But I am not so deluded as to think you cannot explain that" cried the girl. "How foolish! You are not a servant, never were, and I am sure never will be one. And I know you have n't sneaked in as a yellow newspaper reporter, or magazine writer," tentatively. "You are not a sneak."

"No, I have not the intention, nor the ability, to make copy of my experiences," said Armitage.

"Intention!" echoed the girl. "Well, since you suggest the word, just what was, or is, your intention then?—if I may ask."

Armitage straightened and looked full at the girl.

"Suppose I should say that ever since that morning on the *General* I had—" Armitage hesitated. "I reckon I 'd rather not say that," he added.

"No, I reckon you had better not," she said placidly. "In the meantime, how long do you intend staying with us before giving notice?"

Armitage did not reply immediately. He stood for a moment in deep thought. When he looked up his face was serious.

"Miss Wellington, I have neither done nor said anything that would lead you to believe that, whatever I may have been, I am now in any way above what I appear to be, with the Wellington livery on my back. I say this in justice to you. I say it because I am grateful to you. You may regard it as a warning, if you will."

For a moment she did not reply, sitting rigidly thoughtful, while Armitage, abandoning all pretence at work, stood watching her.

"Very well," she said at length, and her voice was coldly conventional. "If you have finished your repairs, will you drive me to Mrs. Van Valkenberg's? Follow this road through; turn to your left, and I 'll tell you when to stop."

Sara Van Valkenberg was one of the most popular of the younger matrons of Newport and New York. As Sara Malalieu, daughter of a prime old family, Billy Van Valkenberg had discovered her, and their wedding had been an event from which many good people in her native city dated things. Van Valkenberg was immensely wealthy and immensely wicked. Sara had not sounded the black depths of his character when he was killed in a drunken automobile ride two years before, but she had learned enough to appreciate the kindness of an intervening fate.

Now she lived in an Elizabethan cottage sequestered among the rocks a short distance inland from the Ocean Drive. She was very good to look at, very worldly wise, and very, very popular. She was thirty years old, an age not to be despised in a woman.

When Miss Wellington's car arrived at the cottage, Tommy Osgood's motor was in front of the door, which was but a few feet from the road. With an expression of annoyance, Anne ran up the steps and rang the bell. The footman was about to take her card when Mrs. Van Valkenberg's voice sounded from the library.

"Come in, Anne, we saw you coming."

Anne entered the apartment and found her friend reclining in all her supple ease, watching flushed-face Tommy, who had been attempting to summon his nerve to tell her how little he cared to continue his course through the world without her, which was just what she did not wish to have him do, because Tommy was a manly, likable, unassuming chap and had much yet to learn, being several years her junior.

"Oh, Tommy," said Anne, "I wanted to speak to Sara alone for a moment."

"Tommy was on his way to the polo field," said Mrs. Van Valkenberg, suggestively. "Now he need have no further excuse for being civil to an old lady."

"By George," said Tommy, "that's so, I must be on my way." And he went, not without some confusion.

Sara watched him through the window as he walked to his car.

"Poor, dear boy," she said. She turned to Anne with a bright smile. "What is it, dear?"

"Prince Koltsoff is with us, as you know. I think mother would be pleased if I married him. I don't know that I am not inclined to gratify her. I have n't talked to father yet."

"Then he has not told you about the Russian railroad thingamajigs he is gunning for?" asked Mrs. Van Valkenberg.

"Really!" Anne's eyes were very wide.

"Oh, I don't know anything about it," said Sara hastily. "Only—the men were speaking of it at the Van Antwerps', the other night. And how about Koltsoff?"

"His intentions are distressingly clear," said Anne.

Mrs. Van Valkenberg whistled.

"Congratulations," she said with an upward inflection. "You 've no idea—"

"Oh, sh's'sh!" exclaimed Anne. "Don't try to be enthusiastic if you find it so difficult. Anyway, there will be nothing to justify enthusiasm if I can help it."

"Really!" Sara regarded the girl narrowly. "If you can help it! What do you mean?"

"I don't know exactly what I do mean," Anne laughed nervously. "He is so thrillingly dominant. He had not been in the house much more than thirty hours before he had lectured me on the narrowness of my life, indicated a more alluring future, kissed my hand, and reposed in me a trust upon which he said his future depended. And through all I have been as a school girl. He 's fascinating, Sara." She leaned forward and placed her hand upon her friend's knee. "Sara—now don't laugh, I 'm serious—"

"I'm not going to laugh, dear; go on."

"Sara, you know the world.... I thought I did, don't you know. But I 'm a child, a perfect simpleton. I said Prince Koltsoff was fascinating; I meant he fascinates me. He does really. Some time when he gets under full headway he is going to take me in his arms—that's the feeling; also that I shall let him, although the idea now fills me with dread."

"Why, Anne!"

"I know," continued the girl, "isn't it too absurd for words! But I am baring my soul. Do you marry a man because his eyes seem to draw you into them?—whose hand pressure seems to melt your will? Is that love?"

Sara regarded the girl for a few minutes without speaking. Then she lifted her brows.

"*Is* it love?" she said. "Ask yourself."

Anne shrugged her shoulders and grimaced helplessly.

"It might be, after all," she said. "I am sure I don't know."

"Yes, it might be," smiled Sara; "it's a question in which you must consider the personal equation. I am rather finicky about men who exude what seems to pass for love. They don't make good husbands. The best husband is the one who wins you, not takes you. For heaven's sake, Anne, when you marry, let your romance be clean, wholesome, natural; not a demonstration in psychic phenomena, to use a polite term."

Anne smiled.

"Oh, it is n't as bad as that. I—I—oh, I don't know what to say, Sara. His family, don't you know, are really high in Russia, and Koltsoff himself is close to the reigning family, as his father and grandfather were before him. It is rather exciting to think of the opportunity—" Anne paused and gazed at the older woman with feverish eyes. "And yet," she added, "I never before thought of things in this way. I have always been quite content that coronets and jewelled court gowns and kings and emperors and dukes and," she smiled, "princes, should fall to the lot of other women. I am afraid I have been too much of an American—in spite of mother—"

"Who really underneath is a better American than any of us," said Mrs. Van Valkenberg. She had arisen and was standing looking out of the window, toying with the silken fringe of the curtain. "There's hope for you, Anne.... Of course I shan't advise you. I could n't, don't you know, not knowing Prince Koltsoff." She paused and gazed eagerly in the direction of Anne's car. Her lips framed an exclamation, but she checked it. "By-the-bye, Anne," she said, "I see you have a new driver."

Anne nodded absently.

"Yes. Mother employed him this morning as physical instructor to the boys and I commandeered him—I believe that's the word—because Rimini is in New York and Benoir tried to knock down a telegraph pole and is in the hospital."

"What a find!" observed Mrs. Van Valkenberg. "And yet how curious!" Suddenly she turned to the girl.

"Anne, I am going to be dreadful and you must be honest with me. You know you asked me to go to you the middle of the week to stay over the *fête*. May I come now—today? I cannot tell you why I ask now, but when I do you will be interested. May I? I know I am preposterous."

"Preposterous! How absurd! Certainly, you may. You will do nicely as a chaperon. Mother, I am afraid, is going to insist upon all the conventions. You must know how delighted I am." She kissed her enthusiastically. "We will expect you at dinner?" she said tentatively. "Or will you come with me now?" She thought a second. "I don't know whether I told you I was to take Prince Koltsoff motoring this afternoon—unchaperoned."

"Why, Anne, if you are going to bother about me that way, I 'll withdraw my request. Please don't let me interfere in any way. I couldn't possibly go before late in the afternoon, in any event."

"That will be fine then," said Anne, holding out her hand. "*Au revoir.* I 'll send the car for you after we return."

After she had gone, Mrs. Van Valkenberg stood watching the car until it disappeared, and then snatching her bright-eyed Pomeranian, she ran her fingers absently through his soft hair.

"How ridiculous," she said, "how absolutely ridiculous!"

CHAPTER XII
MISS HATCH SHOWS SHE LOVES A LOVER

When Armitage entered the servants' dining-room he found the head footman, who presided, in something of a quandary as to where he should place him. Emilia, Miss Wellington's maid, had of course lost no time in imparting to all with whom she was on terms of confidence, that the new chauffeur was the same with whom her mistress had flirted on the *General*. Consequently, Armitage was at once the object of interest, suspicion, respect, and jealousy. But the head footman greeted him cordially enough and after shifting and rearranging seats, indicated a chair near the lower end of the table, which Armitage accepted with a nod. He was immensely interested.

The talk was of cricket. Some of the cottagers whose main object in life was aping the ways of the English, had organized a cricket team, and as there were not enough of them for an opposing eight, they had been compelled to resort to the grooms. There were weekly matches in which the hirelings invariably triumphed. One of the Wellington grooms, an alert young cockney, was the bowler, and his success, as well as the distinguished social station of his opponents, appeared to Armitage to have quite turned his pert little head.

There was a pretty Irish chambermaid at Jack's elbow whose eyes were as gray as the stones in the Giants' Causeway, but glittering now with scorn. For heretofore, Henry Phipps had been an humble worshipper. She permitted several of his condescending remarks to pass without notice, but finally when he answered a question put by another groom with a bored monosyllable, the girl flew to the latter's defence.

"'Yes' and 'no,' is it?" she blazed. "Henry Phipps, ye 're like the ass in the colored skin—not half as proud as ye 're painted. A bowler, ye are! But ye take yer hat off after the game, just the same, and bowl out yer masters with a 'thank ye, sur; my misthake!' Ye grovellin' thing, ya!"

"Really," yawned Henry in his rich dialect.

"Really!" mocked the girl. "I could give ye talk about a real Prince—none of yer Rensselaers or Van Antwerps and the like—had I—"

Armitage leaned forward, but anything more the maid might have been tempted to say was interrupted by a footman from the superintendent's table.

"Mr. Dawson says you 're to come to his table," he said nodding to Armitage, who arose with real reluctance, not because of any desire for intimate knowledge of the servants' hall, but because he had decided he could use the Irish maid to the ends he had in view. Now that lead was closed for the time at least and he took his place at the side of the decorous butler, uncheered by Mr. Dawson's announcement that Miss Wellington had ordered his promotion.

"It was very good of Miss Wellington," he said in a perfunctory manner.

"Oh, not at all," replied the butler. "Frequently the chauffeur sits at our table." He shrugged his shoulders. "It depends upon the manner of men. They are of all sorts and constantly changing."

Armitage glanced at Buchan and grinned.

"Thanks," he said.

The butler nodded and then *apropos* of some thought passing through his mind he glanced tentatively at the housekeeper.

"We 'll wake up, I suppose, with the Prince here. I hope so. I have never seen everybody in Newport so quiet."

"Yes, I imagine so," replied Mrs. Stetson. "Several are coming the middle of the week and of course you know of the Flower Ball for Friday night."

"Of course," said the butler, who a second later belied his assumption of knowledge by muttering, "Flower Ball, eh! Gracious, I wonder what won't Mrs. Wellington be up to next!"

"I don't think I like Prince Koltsoff," said Miss Hatch.

"Well," agreed the superintendent, "he's a Russian."

"Oh, I don't care about *that*," replied the young woman. "He is going to marry Miss Wellington—and he 's not the man for her. He 's not the man for any girl as nice as Anne Wellington. Think of it. Ugh!"

"So!" interjected the tutor, Dumois, who had turned many a dollar supplying the newspapers with information, for which they had been willing to pay liberally. "International alliance! How interesting. The latest, eh?"

"No, it's not the latest," replied the secretary. "If it were, I should have said nothing. It's only a baseless fear; but a potent one."

"Oh," Dumois turned ruefully to his plate.

"He attracts her," resumed the secretary.

"That is to be seen plainly—and she attracts him. That is as far as it has gone."

"That is quite far," observed the tutor, glancing up hopefully.

"Oh, no," said Armitage warmly. He paused, and then finding every one looking at him he applied himself to his luncheon not without confusion.

"I wish I could agree with you," sighed Miss Hatch. "She is a dear girl. But you don't understand girls of her class. They have the queerest ideas."

"Oh, I don't think they differ from other girls," said Mrs. Stetson. "It is merely that they have the actual opportunity for realizing what to other girls are mere dreams. I can imagine what my daughter would have done if a foreign nobleman had paid court to her. I will say this for Miss Wellington though; she would marry her chauffeur if she took the whim."

Armitage, caught off his guard, looked up quickly.

"You don't say!" he exclaimed, whereat every one laughed and Dawson shook his head in mock seriousness at him.

"See here, young man, if you make an attempt to demonstrate Mrs. Stetson's theory, Ronald Wellington will drive you out of the country."

Armitage laughed.

"Well," he said, "I'll pick Vienna."

As they were leaving the table, Miss Hatch caught Armitage's eye. She had lingered behind the rest, bending over some ferns which showed signs of languishing. Her eyeglasses glittered humorously at Armitage as he sauntered carelessly to her side.

"It is all right, Mr. McCall," she said.

"All right?"

"I mean the incident in the garage. Master Ronald applied vigorously for your discharge."

Armitage smiled.

"I imagined he would. The application was not sustained?"

"Hardly. At first, of course, Mrs. Wellington was quite indignant. Then Miss Wellington came in and really she was a perfect fury in your behalf. She made Master Ronald confess he had been smoking and showed quite clearly that you were right."

"Bully for her! As a matter of fact, I don't think it was any of my business. But that chap got on my nerves."

"He gets on all our nerves. But I'm quite sure he's all right at heart. It's a disagreeable age in a boy." She paused and gazed steadily at Armitage for a second. "I cannot imagine why you are here, Mr. McCall. And yet—and yet, I wonder." She shrugged her shoulders. "Pray don't think me rude," she said and smiled, "but I really am—hoping. I can read Anne Wellington at times, and you—oh, I *am* rude—but I seem to read you like an open book."

Armitage was looking at her curiously, but obviously he was not offended. She stepped towards him impulsively.

"Oh, Mr. Arm—McCall—" she stopped, blushing confusedly.

The break was too much even for Armitage's presence of mind. He jerked his head upward, then collecting himself resumed his expression of amused interest. The secretary made no attempt to dissemble her agitation.

"I am so sorry," she said, "but you must know now that I know whom you are."

Never in his life had Jack felt quite so ill at ease, or so utterly foolish.

"Who else knows?" he asked lamely.

"Only one, beside myself—Mrs. Wellington."

"Mrs. Wellington!"

"Naturally," said Miss Hatch placidly. "Did you suppose for a moment you could successfully hide anything from her? Chief Roberts was in the house an hour after you were employed."

"Oh!" A great white light illumined Jack's mind. He turned to the woman eagerly. "Do you know what Roberts told her?"

"Why, everything, I imagine," said Miss Hatch, laughing.

"Everything! But what?" Armitage gestured impatiently. "Please don't think me inquisitive, but I must know—it will depend upon what our loquacious chief said, whether I stay here one more minute."

"The chief was not loquacious," smiled Miss Hatch. "He was quite the reverse. You would have enjoyed the grilling Mrs. Wellington gave him. He was no willing witness, but finally admitted you were a naval officer, a son of Senator Armitage, and that you were here to observe the actions of one of the grooms, formerly in the Navy, whom the Government thought needed watching."

Inwardly relieved, Armitage grinned broadly.

"I like that chief," he said. "He is so secretive. But Mrs. Wellington can't be pleased at having a Navy man masquerading about. Why hasn't she discharged me?"

"I can't imagine," said Miss Hatch frankly, "unless—yes, I think she has taken a liking to you. Then, for a woman of her mental processes, discharging you off-hand, come to think of it, would be the one thing she would not do. I think she is interested in awaiting developments. I am sure of it, for she commanded me to speak to no one concerning your identity."

"Miss Wellington?" Armitage looked at the woman quickly.

"Her daughter was very particularly included in the orders Mrs. Wellington gave."

Armitage made no attempt to conceal the pleasure this statement gave him. Then a thought occurred to him.

"By the way," he said, looking at Miss Hatch keenly, "if I recall, you said you could not imagine why I am here. In view of all you have told me, why could n't you?"

Miss Hatch turned and walked toward the door. At the sill she glanced back over her shoulder and smiled significantly.

"Oh, that was an introductory figure of speech," she said. "I think, I think I can—imagine."

Then she turned and walking along the hall, with Armitage following, she sang as though to herself:

> "In days of old when knights were bold
> And barons held their sway,
> A warrior bold with spurs of gold
> Sang merrily his lay.
> 'Oh, what care I though death be nigh,
> For love—'"

But Armitage had disappeared.

> "Oh, the little more and how much it is,
> And the little less and what worlds away."

CHAPTER XIII
ANNE EXHIBITS THE PRINCE

Prince Koltsoff had enjoyed his luncheon, as only an exacting gourmet whose every canon of taste has been satisfied, can. His appetite was a many-stringed instrument upon which only the most gifted culinary artist could play. Now as he sat dallying daintily with his *compote* of pears it was patent that Rambon, the Wellington chef, had achieved a dietary symphony.

"Mrs. Wellington," he said at length, "you have a *saucier par excellence*. That *sauce de cavitar*! If I may say so, it lingers. Who is he? It seems almost—yet it cannot be true—that I recognize the genius of Jules Rambon."

"Very well done, Prince Koltsoff," replied Mrs. Wellington, employing phraseology more noncommittal than Koltsoff realized.

Anne, who had been gazing languidly out a window giving on Brenton's Reef lightship, where several black torpedo boats and destroyers were manoeuvring, smiled and glanced at the Prince.

"You have the instincts of a virtuoso. That was really clever of you. The Duchess d'Izes sent him to mother two years ago. You must speak to him. I 'm afraid he feels he is not altogether appreciated here."

The Prince raised his hands.

"What a fate!" he exclaimed. "When Rambon was *chef* for President Carnot, kings and emperors bestowed upon him decorations. I recall that when he created the *Parfait Rambon*—ah!—the governor of his Province set aside a day of celebration. Rambon unappreciated—it is to say that genius is unappreciated!" He turned apologetically to Mrs. Wellington. "America—what would you?"

Mrs. Wellington sniffed ever so slightly. She had become a bit weary of the Russian's assumption of European superiority. She recognized that in Prince Koltsoff she had a guest, her possession of whom had excited among the cottage colony the envy of all those whose envy she desired. So far as she was concerned, that was all she wanted. Now that Anne and the Prince appeared to be hitting it off, she was content to let that matter take its course as might be, with, however, a pretty well defined conviction that her daughter was thoroughly alive to the desirability, not to say convenience, of such an alliance. In her secret heart, however, she rather marvelled at Anne's open interest in the Koltsoff. To be frank, the Prince was boring her and she had come to admit that she, personally, had far rather contemplate the noble guest as a far-distant son-in-law, than as a husband, assuming that her age and position were eligible.

So—she sniffed.

"My dear Prince," she said, "I will take you to a hundred tables in Newport and—I was going to say ten thousand—a thousand in New York, where the food is better cooked than in any private house in Europe."

Touched upon a spot peculiarly tender, Koltsoff all but exploded.

"*Pouf!*" he cried. Then he laughed heartily. "You jest, surely, my dear madame."

"No, I fancy not," replied Mrs. Wellington placidly.

"Oh, but how can you know! Where is it that the writings of Careme are studied and known? Where is it that the memory of Beauvilliers and the reputations of Ranhofer and Casimir and Mollard are preserved? In Europe—"

"In Paris," corrected Mrs. Wellington.

"Well. And from Paris disseminated glowingly throughout Europe—'"

"And the United States."

Koltsoff struggled with himself for a moment.

"Pardon," he said, "but, bah! It cannot be."

"Naturally, you are at the disadvantage of not having had the experience at American tables that I have had abroad," observed Mrs. Wellington rising. "But we shall hope to correct that while you are here.... As for the sauce you praised, it was not by Rambon—who is out to-day—but by Takakika, his assistant, a Japanese whom Mr. Wellington brought on from the Bohemian Club, I think, in San Francisco."

If Koltsoff did not catch Mrs. Wellington's intimation that he must have learned of the presence of Rambon in her kitchen,—which might have been more accurately described as a laboratory,—Anne Wellington did, and she hastened to intervene.

"Oh, Prince Koltsoff," she said, "I have been so interested in those torpedo boats out there. They 've been dashing about the lightship all through lunch. What is the idea, do you know?"

The Prince glanced out of the window.

"I cannot imagine." He gazed over the ocean in silence for several minutes. "Have you a telescope?" he said at length.

Anne nodded.

"The large glass is on that veranda. And you 'll excuse me until half after three, won't you?"

"Until half after three," said the Prince, still rather ruffled as the result of his duel with the mother.

Then he went out on the porch and for an hour had the torpedo boats under his almost continuous gaze.

"Nothing but hide and seek," he muttered as he finally snapped the shutter of the glass and went to his room to dress.

He had quite recovered his spirits when he handed Anne Wellington into the motor car. Armitage had half turned and she caught his eyes. Just the faintest suspicion of a smile appeared on her face as she leaned forward.

"Along the Ocean Drive, McCall, down Bellevue Avenue, past Easton's Beach, and out through Paradise. Drive slowly, please."

Armitage touched his cap and the car was soon rolling along the Ocean Drive. They had not turned Bateman's Point when Anne had proof of the interest which the advent of the Prince had excited among her set. The Wadsworth girls with young Pembroke, Delaney Drew on horseback, and several others were gathered on the grass of the Point, watching the finish of the race for the Astor cups off Brenton's Reef. As the Wellington car rolled slowly by, every one withdrew attention from the exciting finish which three of the yachts were making, and gazed so hard at the Prince that some of them forgot to return Anne's nod. But the girl understood and smiled inwardly, not altogether without pride.

On Bellevue Avenue old Mrs. Cunningham-Jones all but fell out of her carriage, while Minnie Rensselaer, who had been cool lately, was all smiles. And the entrance to the Casino, as Miss Wellington afterward described it, might have been pictured as one great staring eye.

She did not attempt to deny to herself that she was enjoying all this. She was a normal girl with a normal girl's love of distinction and of things that thrill pleasurably. She left nothing undone to heighten the effect she and the Prince, or the Prince and she, were creating. Mrs. Rensselaer saw her gazing into the face of her guest with kindling eyes. "Old Lady" Cunningham-Jones saw her touch his arm to emphasize a remark.

Whatever may have been the exact degree of Koltsoff's attractions for Anne, it was certain that in the course of the drive, thus far, the situation and not the Russian's personality constituted the strong appeal. The girl was far from a snob and yet this—yes, public parading—of a man whose prospective sojourn in Newport had excited so many tea tables for the past fortnight, had furnished so much pabulum for the digestion of society journalists, involved many elements that appealed to her. Chiefly, it must be confessed, she saw the humor of it; otherwise pride might have obtained mastery—there was pride, of course. There was a whirl of things, in fact, and all enjoyable; also, perhaps, a trifle upsetting, inasmuch as her assumption of more than friendly interest in her guest was not altogether the part of wisdom.

The Prince was elated, exalted. It would not have taken a close observer to decide that in his devotion there was no element of the spurious and in his happiness, no flaw. As for Armitage, unseeing, but sensing clearly the drift of things, his eyes were grimly fixed ahead, the muscles of his jaws bulging in knots on either side. This chauffeur business, he felt, was fast becoming a bore.

As he started to turn the corner of the Casino block, Anne, seized by a sudden inspiration, ordered him to back around to the entrance.

"Would n't you like to stop in the Casino for a few minutes and meet a few people?" she asked, smiling at Koltsoff.

The Prince would be only too happy to do anything that Miss Wellington suggested, and so with a warning *honk! honk!* Armitage ran his car up to the curb. At their side the tide of motor cars, broughams, victorias, coaches, jaunting cars and what not swept unceasingly by. Three sight-seeing barges had paused in their "twelve miles for fifty cents" journey around the island. As the Prince and Anne alighted, a small body of curious loiterers moved forward, among them several photographers, seeing which, Anne lowered an opaque veil over her face, a precaution which the beautiful or famous or notorious of the Newport colony invariably find necessary when abroad.

The sight-seeing drivers, with whips poised eagerly, viewed the alighting couple and then turning to their convoy, announced in voices not too subdued:

"Miss Anne Wellington, daughter of Ronald Wellington, the great railroad magnate, and the Prince of Rooshia are just gettin' out," indicating the car with their whips. "They say they 're engaged to be married—so far only a rumor. Miss Wellington is the one who put little pinchin' crabs in Mrs. Minnie Rensselaer's finger bowls last year and made a coolness between these two great families."

Miss Wellington, whose cheeks felt as though they would burn her veil, saw Armitage's shoulders quivering with some emotion, as she hurried from the sidewalk into the doorway of the low, dark-shingled building and out into the circle of trim lawn and garden.

There were groups around a few of the tables in the two tiers of the encircling promenade, but Anne did not know any of them. They strolled on to a passageway under the structure leading to several acres of impeccable lawn, with seats under spreading trees and tennis courts on all sides. An orchestra was playing Handel's "Largo." The low hanging branches sheltered many groups, dotting the green with vivid color notes. A woman with gray veil thrown back and with a wonderful white gown held court under a spreading maple, half a dozen gallants in white flannels paying homage. All about were gowns of white, of pink, of blue, of light green, Dresden colors, tones of rare delicacy mingling with the emerald turf and the deeper green of the foliage. The spell of mid-summer was everywhere present. To Anne it seemed as if the Summer would last for always and that the Casino would never be deserted again, the grass sere and brown or piled with drifts of snow.

"Isn't it beautiful!" she exclaimed, as the Prince shook his head negatively at a red-coated page with an armful of camp chairs.

"The women," smiled the Prince, "they are superb! I concede freely the supremacy of the American girl." He paused, "It *is* beautiful. Yet certainly, what place would not be beautiful where you are, Miss Wellington! Do I say too much? Ah, how can I say less!" His eyes were suffused with his emotions.

"Don't, please, Prince Koltsoff," she said, lowering her eyes to the turf. "Not here—oh, I mean not—"

"Here! I would willingly kneel here and kiss the hem of your skirt. I should be proud that all should see, Anne.... Ah, let us not dissemble—"

Anne, thoroughly agitated, suddenly faced the Prince.

"Stop! I want you to," she interrupted. "You must. You must not say such things—" she paused, conscious that the eyes of many to whom she had purposed presenting the Prince were turned curiously upon them, although fortunately, from distances comparatively remote. She forced a vivacious smile for the benefit of observers and continued, "You must not say these things until I tell you you may.... Now, please!" as the Prince showed indications of disobeying her wishes.

He kept silence and as some manifestations of sulkiness, not inclined to encourage Anne in her intentions of introducing him generally, revealed themselves, she turned and led the way back to the car, where Armitage sat hunched, in no blithe mood himself.

In plying him with questions as to himself and his deeds, which developed a mood ardently vainglorious, Anne skilfully led Koltsoff's trend of thought from amatory channels. They stopped at Paradise and Anne and the Prince walked from the roadside across a stretch of gorse to a great crevice in the cliffs, known as the "Lover's Leap."

"Here," said the girl, imitating the manner of a guide, "legend says an Indian maiden, very beautiful, was walking with one of her suitors, when a rival accosted them. They drew their knives and were about to fight, when the girl interposed. Pointing to the chasm she declared she would marry the man who first jumped across it."

"Ah, the time-worn lover's leap! They have them in England, Russia, Germany—everywhere. America not to be behind—" the Prince wrinkled his brows. "Let me see how closely the Indians followed their European originals. Did they leap?"

"They did," smiled the girl. "Both, I believe, were killed." She peered into the dark fissure where the waters wound among the crags fifty feet below. "Ugh! What a fall! Their love must have been wonderfully compelling."

"So," replied the Prince, gallantly, "and yet I should do it for a smile from you or at most for a—" he bowed low, seized her hand, and deftly bore it to his lips.

She drew it away hastily, a wave of irritation flushing her face, and a powerful revulsion from her former mood of exaltation took possession of her whole being.

"You have improved upon knights errant of old," she said slowly. "You seize your guerdon before paying your devoir." She pointed to the chasm, which was about eight feet across at the spot where they were standing. "Your lady waits, Sir Knight."

The Prince pushed his hand through his hair and laughed.

"Miss Wellington—indeed, indeed, I appreciate your humor. It is well caught. That is to say—ha, ha! Your father will enjoy your wit."

"I am waiting," said the girl, as though she had not heard. "Knights—and gentlemen do not take from women that which they are not willing to pay for."

"But—" the Prince glanced at the yawning hole. "You surely jest. Why, my dear lady!" The Prince involuntarily stepped backward.

Anne smiled maliciously. Her meaning was clear and the Prince flushed.

"What man would attempt it!" he exclaimed. "What man indeed," he added, "save one who would throw away his life to no purpose. Come, Miss Wellington, I am sure you do not seek my life."

"By no means," said the girl beginning to relent, but still enjoying the success of her *coup*. "But really that is a small leap for a man. My driver, I believe—" Her face suddenly lighted with a new inspiration. Hastily she walked to the top of the bluff. "McCall," she cried. "Will you come here a minute?"

As the two arrived at the chasm, she nodded to the opposite side.

"If you cleared that would it be a remarkable leap?"

Armitage surveyed the gap with his eye, looked behind him and studied the ground.

"Not especially, Miss Wellington, so far as distance is concerned." He had done his nineteen feet in the running broad jump.

"Ah, just so," broke in the Prince. "It is the condition which would follow a slip or mistake in judgment."

Anne shook her head impatiently at Koltsoff's obvious eagerness.

"I do not believe McCall thought of that; nervous systems vary in their intensity."

Some part of the situation Armitage grasped. It was clear that for some reason she had dared the Prince to make the jump and that he had declined. The ground upon which they were standing was a few feet above the rocks on the other side of the chasm and the three stood about a dozen feet from the mouth.

She turned to Armitage.

"Am I right, or do you share Prince Koltsoff's psychological views?"

Koltsoff, who from the beginning had chafed at the position in which she had placed him, pitting him against a servant, walked to one side with a low sibilant exclamation.

"Not at all," said Armitage, and without further words he drew back a few feet and started swiftly for the fissure. Anne, who had not intended that the incident should thus get away from her, acted upon flashing instinct, before the situation could formulate itself in her mind. She sprang at Armitage as he passed her, her hands tightly clasping about his neck, and pulled him backward with all her strength. Armitage half stumbling, stopped, and the girl, releasing her hands, stepped back with a sob of nervous anger.

"You—you—oh, you idiot!" she exclaimed. "How dare you frighten me so! Now—go back to the car!"

"I did not mean to frighten you, Miss Wellington," he replied, not altogether in the mild, impersonal tone of a servant. "It was a perfectly easy jump. I thought you—"

"Go to your car, please," interrupted the girl sternly.

As for Koltsoff, rankling with the knowledge that if he had taken her at her word and essayed to make the leap, she would have prevented him as she had her chauffeur, his mood was no enviable one. Lost opportunities of any sort are not conducive to mental equanimity. He maintained extreme taciturnity throughout the remainder of the drive and Miss Wellington, whose thoughts seemed also absorbing, made no attempt to restore his ardent spirits. When they entered the Wellington driveway, she glanced at Armitage's well-set back and shoulders and smiled.

"McCall," she said, as she stood on the veranda, "I want you to go to Mrs. Van Valkenberg's—where you were this morning—and bring her here. You may have to wait."

CHAPTER XIV
UNDERGROUND WIRES

Armitage was not obliged to wait, however. A tall, well-built young woman, heavily veiled, came down the winding path as he shut off power. When he leaned around to open the door of the tonneau, she threw back her veil and he caught sight of a full, dark, handsome face and eyes filled with a curious light. He slammed the door and turned quickly to the wheel.

"What is your name, my man?" The deep alto voice contained a note of mirth.

"McCall," replied Armitage gruffly, jerking his head a bit side-wise and then jerking it quickly back again.

"You are—not a very good driver," came the voice. "But I should like to employ you.... Would you consider leaving Miss Wellington?"

Armitage shook his head grouchily.

"For a consideration? Come, I won't use you as a chauffeur. I want you for a statue in my Japanese garden. I—"

Armitage suddenly pointed the car toward the ocean and stopped. Then he turned in his seat.

"Look here, Sara," he said, "if you don't let up, I'll run you into the ocean."

Mrs. Van Valkenberg was rocking with laughter.

"Oh, Jack! Jack!" she cried. "This is too rich. What on earth are you up to?"

Armitage, who had not seen her since they had attended school together in Louisville, paid no attention to her question.

"I had no idea you were in Newport."

"I suppose I should expect more of one of my very oldest and best friends," she said.

"I was in the Philippines when you married; faint rumors of the event penetrated even there. I was too prostrated to write; besides, I didn't receive any cards." He paused a moment. "Van Valkenberg—that's so; I remember now. He—"

"I am a widow," said Sara soberly.

"Oh," he was silent, not knowing what to say.

She hastened to relieve his embarrassment, smiling brightly.

"I was to go to see Anne later in the week, but when I saw you, I simply could n't wait another minute. I wanted a front seat at this little comedy. You see," she raised her eyes knowingly, "I have n't asked you why you are here in the Wellington livery and driving the Wellington car because—because I rather imagine I can guess the reason."

She glanced at Armitage, who did not reply.

"Fancy my missing this romance," she went on, laughing musically. "Jack, it's perfectly delightful. It's more than delightful, it's sublimely rich. You, *you* of all men! Come, won't you confide in me? Ah, go on." Her eyes were brimming with laughter.

Armitage frowned.

"Look here, Sara, you're on the wrong tack."

"Oh, is it possible! All right, you need n't confide in me if you don't wish to. All I ask is permission to view events—and you can't withhold that, you know. But seriously, Jack, can I be of any assistance? I approve, don't you know, awfully. And—she's worth every bit of it. But how are you going to win her in the guise of a chauffeur? I always knew you possessed a large amount of self-confidence, but allow me to inform you, sir, there are some things your natural qualifications can't overshadow. Come, Jack, do strip off your motley and court her as a naval officer—you see I, at least, have kept track of *you*—and a gentleman should; I don't like this way."

"I tell you, you are wrong. I can't say anything now. But wait—then you 'll know. And, Sara, please; not a word as to whom I am; promise me you 'll keep still until I give you the word."

She smiled enigmatically.

"Don't you admire Anne Wellington?"

"Come, Sara, promise; this is a serious matter with me."

"Don't you?" she persisted.

"Of course I do," he snapped. "She's a corker. Now promise."

"I promise nothing. I shall act as I think best for you."

Armitage gazed at her thoughtfully for a moment.

"You may trust me, Jack. I may be able to help you. I feel sure I shall. I want to help you—and Anne."

Armitage raised his hand warningly.

"Don't, Sara, please!"

"Very well." She smiled sweetly. "You may proceed to The Crags, McCall."

Anne met her at the doorway and Armitage took the car to the garage.

"Say," said Ryan, "there 's some one been calling you up for the past hour."

Armitage looked at the man excitedly.

"Who was it? Did he give his name?"

"No, would n't give it. He said he 'd call up again, though. He—there goes the bell now."

Armitage took up the receiver.

"Is this you, Jack?" came the voice. "This is Thornton. Say, they 've got Yeasky."

"Where?" Jack's voice was husky.

"In Boston."

"Did they find anything?"

"No; they went through everything. He had n't a thing except a note signed 'Vassili' something, and some Austrian army data."

"The family name of the man we 're gunning for," said Armitage. "Has he said anything?"

"Nothing. They have not told him what he was captured for either, although I guess he knows. They want your orders."

"All right," said Armitage. "Tell them to let him go, provided he leaves Boston by the first boat."

"What!"

"Turn him loose. Get shed of him. It 'll simplify matters. I 'm getting this thing in hand now. Push the thing through for me, will you, Joe? I'm busy as a pup here. Get Bill Rawlins on the long distance at the Boston Navy Yard, explain things to him, and get him to help. There 's nothing to do. Just have him seen on board the boat. That note was all I wanted. Have that sent to me. Now do it all nicely for me, won't you, old chap,—and a day or two will see the finish of the whole thing. Oh, say,—have them hold those papers."

"All right," said Thornton. "By the way, we are going to torpedo the Atlantic fleet tonight. The battleships are on their way down from Provincetown at last."

"Pshaw! The one thing I wanted to be in on!"

"Can't you get off and come along on the *D'Estang*? We shan't leave until eight o'clock. We 're going to try and do up the fleet off Point Jude. Come on, like a good chap."

"I 'd like to. I will if I can, you bet. I think I can work it. Now s'long and don't forget to have that Pole shunted out of the country on the jump."

"I won't. Don't worry; see you later then."

"Right-o, good-bye."

As Armitage hung up the receiver the bell of the house 'phone jingled and Armitage was summoned to bring out the car in a hurry. When he arrived under the *porte cochère*, Prince Koltsoff was still talking to Anne in a corner of the library.

"It is very necessary," he was saying. "The summons is important. It is even possible I shall not return all night." His agitation seemed momentarily increasing.

"But, Prince Koltsoff," said Anne, "is it so very important? I hardly know what to do. I have arranged a box party for the vaudeville at Freebody to-night—it's distressing."

Koltsoff bowed.

"And I! You cannot suppose I view lightly being away from you to-night!" He shrugged his shoulders. "The rose-strewn paths are not always for diplomats. You will know that better in good time, perhaps. But they are for that all the sweeter while we tread them." He moved very close to her and she, taking fire from his mood, did not step backward, looking him in the eyes, pulling slightly at the front of her skirt. In the very web of a mood which she felt bordered on surrender to the masculine personality of the man before her, she admitted a thrill, which she never before had recognized. The blood mounted swiftly to her temples and she straightened and threw her head back with lips parted and hot. His face came so close to hers that she felt his hot breath.

"Are you sorry for this afternoon?" he asked caressingly.

"Yes," her voice was a half whisper.

His arms were raising to take her, when the voice of Sara Van Valkenberg came to their ears, with an effect very much like a cold stream upon a bar of white hot steel.

"Anne, oh, Anne dearie, did you know the car was waiting for Prince Koltsoff?" She appeared in the doorway to find Anne turning over a magazine and the Prince adjusting his coat. "I beg pardon, but you said Prince Koltsoff was in a hurry. I thought you did n't know the car had arrived."

"We—I didn't," Anne smiled thinly. "Thank you."

They moved to the veranda, where Anne and Sara stood with arms intertwined.

"I am sorry, *so* sorry," cried Koltsoff, as he climbed into the car. "As I say, I shall possibly not return all night. At all events, *au revoir*." He turned to Anne and half raised his arm. "The trust," he said. She nodded and smiled.

"Have no fear, Prince Koltsoff," she said.

"Good!" He glared toward Armitage. "To town—and fast," he said.

As Armitage nodded, Anne, whose mood was past praying for, called mischievously:

"McCall, always touch your hat when you receive an order. And come right back, please; I shall want to go to town."

This time Armitage made a faultless salute.

When they had gone, Anne walked to a settee, drawing Mrs. Van Valkenberg by the arm, and flung herself down, laughing hysterically.

"Why, what *is* the matter, Anne?" Sara gazed at her in amazement. "Has anything—" she paused significantly—"happened?"

Anne drew her handkerchief across her eyes.

"No," she said, "not yet. But oh, Sara, if you had n't—" She stopped and gazed at her friend wide-eyed. "Sara," she said, "is it possible I love Prince Koltsoff?"

"No, it is not," replied Sara, decidedly. "Anne, don't be a goose. What is it, tell me?"

"I cannot; but yes, I think it is—it must be. Oh, I wonder!"

"Anne!"

"Sara, for goodness' sake, let me alone a moment. Come," she added, throwing her arm about the young matron's waist, "let's talk about other things now. Come with me while I telephone and call off that stupid theatre party. Then we 'll go to town, exchange the tickets, and then—Sara, let's have a regular bat—alone. You know—one of our old ones. I dare you."

"Done," said Mrs. Van Valkenberg, thankful to change the girl's mood.

While Anne was telephoning and offering various explanations to various persons, Sara sat thinking. It had not taken her ten minutes to decide that she detested Koltsoff and that Anne was under a spell not easily to be broken. If Armitage had tried to break it, if he were there for that purpose, he had failed a long way of success. He had chosen, in any event, a poor method of campaigning. If he did not know what was good for him, so much the worse. She did and accordingly when Anne had finished with the last of her list of prospective guests, she said:

"Anne, I have fallen quite in love with your new chauffeur."

"I don't blame you one bit," said Anne carelessly. "He's a stunner. But I don't believe he 's a chauffeur by profession."

"I happen to know he is n't."

"You—know—he is n't! How do you know? Tell me what he is then. I don't believe I 'll ever have any more curiosity about anything; I 've used it all on him."

"He 's a naval officer and a very promising one, I believe. He is John Armitage and his father is United States Senator Armitage from Kentucky—they 're really a very fine family—one of the best in the State."

"How did—? oh, of course, you were a Kentuckian. You don't mean to say you know him!"

"I know all his family very well. Why, I 've known Jack Armitage all my life," she raised her eyebrows. "But, Anne, promise you won't let on."

The full significance of the information imparted by her friend gradually rose to supremacy in Anne's mind. Her eyes turned slowly to Sara's face.

"Well, of all idiots I am the worst! Why, I even placed him at Annapolis and then let him turn me off! And mother, too! That's a good one on her. Well! What's his play? I confess I am stumped."

"His play?" Sara regarded her with a significant smile. "I wonder!"

Anne gazed at her a moment and then buried her face in her hands with a mock groan.

"Saints and ministers of grace, defend us!" she exclaimed.

Then girl-like, they clung to each other and laughed and laughed.

"Aren't you flattered?" asked Sara at length.

"Flattered? Oh, you mean about—" she grimaced. "Sara! It's perfectly ridiculous! And it is n't true. The very idea! The audacity! Don't tell me, Sara; there 's something else." But Sara caught the tentative note.

"Oh, naturally," she interposed, "you are far from being sufficiently attractive to draw an ardent young man into a romantic situation, especially—as you told me—after you had written him a note virtually inviting him to try his luck."

"Sara, you are beastly!"

"Forgive me, dear, but why not face facts?"

"Well!" Anne smiled resignedly. "Mother must n't know."

"Not until the play is over," said Sara.

Anne gazed moodily at her friend.

"It soon will be, I fear," she said.

As for the unsuspecting Armitage, he burned the road, smiling to think that underground wires were working for him, as well as the Prince. He had no fear that if Koltsoff had the control with him—which Armitage did not for a moment believe—the vigilance of the express companies and of the postal authorities would be found wanting. Koltsoff spent half an hour in the telegraph office and then alighting from the car in Touro Park, bade Armitage return to The Crags.

"Shall I call anywhere for you?" asked Armitage pleasantly.

"No," replied Koltsoff, who stood on the sidewalk, watching until the car disappeared.

CHAPTER XV
ANNE AND SARA SEEK ADVENTURE

"Anne," said Mrs. Wellington, as she came in from her drive a few minutes later, "your chauffeur drives too fast. The car passed me, cutting through Brenton Road a while ago, at a perfectly insane pace. Some one— how do you do, Sara, I 'm delighted to have you with us—was in the tonneau, whom I took to be Koltsoff, although there was such a blur I was n't certain. Was it he?"

"Yes, mother," Anne glanced at Sara. "Isn't it maddening! Some urgent summons, he said, made it necessary for him to go; and he may be away all night. Of course that punctured the party at Freebody."

"It is maddening," Sara hastened to observe.

Mrs. Wellington compressed her lips.

"I had told him your father would arrive this evening. But of course he must have failed to remember that. Fortunately, he will not come on from New York until to-morrow—I 've had a wire. Have you any idea the Prince will be with us to-morrow? Sir Arthur Baddeley will be down from Bar Harbor for the week; Bob Marie is coming with your father, and two or three of the Tuxedo crowd, Sallie and Blanche Turnure and Willie Whipple will be here by Wednesday for the ball, certainly."

"I don't know, really," said Anne, "but I imagine so, of course."

Sara gazed at Mrs. Wellington curiously. It was true the woman was outwardly unperturbed, characteristically so, but Sara had never before been able to read in that mask-like face so many indications of inward irritation. Anne's sly glance told her that she, too, had been able to enjoy a rare opportunity of penetrating beneath the surface.

Mrs. Wellington toyed with her lorgnette for a moment.

"Anne, if Koltsoff returns and I don't see him, let me know the very first minute, will you, please?" She glanced at the girl with an expression best described as detached. "If it interests you any, my daughter, you succeeded in making a sensation this afternoon—you and Koltsoff. I gather that everything was done but placarding him; and I have heard of at least eight persons you cut in the Casino."

"Oh—mother, by the way, if I am not too inquisitive," said Anne, hastening to change the trend of thought, "I read, or heard, somewhere that father was interested in getting hold of a Russian issue of railroad bonds, or something of the sort. Is Prince Koltsoff concerned?"

"Your father has no business dealings with him. Dismiss that thought. Railroad bonds—I believe he was looking into them. I don't know the details, or rather do not recall them. I do remember, though, his saying that he had relinquished the opportunity to the French with great pleasure."

"Oh," said Anne, "I imagined his visit here was a mingling of business with pleasure."

"I don't know what it is a mingling of, I 'm quite sure," said Mrs. Wellington. She turned to go. "I 'm dining out to-night, at the Cunningham-Jones'. I shouldn't have accepted, but you were to be at Berger's with your theatre party. You won't mind, Sara?"

"Not at all, Mrs. Wellington, don't bother about me. I hope I 'm not company."

Mrs. Wellington smiled. She was very partial to the young widow.

"The boys are at Ochre Point for the night. You might call up people if you want company for dinner, Anne."

"To think," cried Anne, as her mother left the room, "how events have shaped themselves for us! Of course we shan't dine at home; I 'll have Emilia tell Mrs. Stetson after we have gone. Now, Sara, what can we do exciting?" Her eyes flashed with animation as she gazed at her friend. "Shall it be shop girl disguises with dinner on Thames Street, or what?"

"I know," cried Sara. "We 'll put on shirt-waist suits and plain hats, muss our hair a bit, and take a trip on a sight-seeing barge."

"Lovely. Mc—Mr. Armitage can take us to the starting place at Easton's Beach and then pick us up there when we get back. After that—"

"Hoop-la," laughed Sara, and the two young women—nothing but school girls now—fell into each other's arms, hugging joyously.

When Armitage appeared again at the *porte cochère* a few minutes before five o'clock, two very changed, but merry young women awaited him. Anne flashed her eyes at Armitage.

"To Easton's Beach, McCall," she said sweetly.

Easton's Beach was at the height of the day's exodus of excursionists to Providence, Fall River, Taunton and elsewhere, as Armitage drew alongside the sun-baked board walk in front of the main bathing pavilion. Trolley cars, which had rolled empty down the long hill by the ocean side, were now ascending laden to the guards, and the ocean, relieved of its bathers, whose suits of multifarious cuts and colors had grievously marred the blue waters, had recovered its beautiful serenity.

"We are going to take a barge ride, McCall," said Anne, as they alighted from the car. "You might follow us at a respectful distance, though, so you can pick us up when we decide to get out."

Armitage touched his cap and sat watching amusedly, while Anne and Sara with exaggerated swinging strides walked toward a barge comfortably filled with a heterogeneous assemblage of sightseers. They paused uncertainly at the side of the clumsy vehicle and were thus espied by the driver, who was on the point of starting his horses.

"Whoa!" he cried, pulling at the reins. "Here you are, ladies. Two seats in the front for the sunset drive. Last chance of the day. All the way round for fifty cents. All points pointed out, with inside information."

Sara glanced doubtfully at Anne, but the girl already had her foot on the step.

"We ain't going all the way," she said. "Can we get out where we please?"

"Sure, the sooner the better," cried the driver cheerfully.

"All right," said Anne, clambering in; "come on, Jane."

Sara followed obediently, kneeing her way along the seat to Anne's side.

"The Cliff Walk," said the driver, swinging his whip to the left as they drove up the hill.

"Is that where society people walk?" asked Anne.

"Naw, only the common people," replied the oracle. "Any society person found there would be ostracized."

"They would!" exclaimed an elderly Irishman, smoking a pipe at Anne's side. "Is th' ground too poor fur their phroud feet?"

"Only think," said a stout woman behind them, leaning forward, "the cottage owners have been tryin' to close up the walk to the public. My brother 's a grocer clerk here and he says the city would be better off without the cottagers. They 're awful! Don't pay their bills and such carryin's on—you 've no idea."

"Use n't you to live here?" asked Sara. "I thought I seen you in the city."

"Not me. I live over to Jamestown," said the stout woman.

In the meantime, Anne had noted to her disgust that two men in white duck trousers and straw yachting caps were trying to catch their attention.

It was not to be wondered at, for despite the broad-brimmed hats tilted well over their foreheads and hair in studied disarray, by way of disguise, no more dashing pair had ever patronized Newport's sightseeing system. Of course this aspect of their adventure had not occurred to Anne and she was about to pull Sara's skirt and suggest that they abandon the trip forthwith, when that young woman glancing about for fresh material, suddenly turned pale.

"Anne!" she whispered. "For heaven's sake! There's my cook at the other end of that back seat—the fat, red-headed man. What shall I do?"

Anne, without replying, touched the driver and handed him a two-dollar bill.

"Keep that," she said, "and please let us out at once."

And so, just a bit panic-stricken, but with ardor undimmed, the two awaited the motor car.

"We might have known!" observed Sara. "Do you suppose he recognized me?"

Anne was laughing.

"How in the world could he help it?"

"Of course," said Sara, her face lighting with the humor of the incident. "I shan't care at all, provided he does n't give me notice."

They were quite ready for Armitage when he came up in the car.

"Where to now, Sara?" Anne stamped her foot. "Isn't that the way! When you have the opportunity and the desire for a good time you can't imagine what to do."

"Well, let us get into the car, anyway," said Sara, "those detestable creatures who were in the barge have actually followed us."

So they entered the motor. Armitage turned inquiringly, but Anne shook her head.

"One moment, if you please."

"I wanted to ask you, Miss Wellington, if you thought I could get away to-night about seven o'clock?" He glared defiantly at Sara, who was ostentatiously concealing her face in her hand. "I have rather an important engagement."

"Why—" Anne glanced at Sara, who seeing an opening for a new avenue of fun, was now laughing unreservedly.

"You really can't think of it, you know, dear," she said. "Why, at seven o'clock he will just begin to be useful."

Anne saw the chauffeur's shoulders shrug angrily, and it amused her.

"Cut through here and drive toward the Training Station," she commanded, "and we 'll think about seven o'clock, McCall."

Sara, who had been vigorously nodding and screwing up her eyes at Armitage's back, laughed musically.

"Anne," she said, "your chauffeur is badly trained as to manners. Really, he suggests a man graduated from the Fifth Avenue buses, don't you know."

"You must make allowances, Sara; he's only an improvised chauffeur."

"I know; but he 's hardly of the chauffeur type. Now as a detective—can't you imagine him in a pair of false whiskers?"

"I 've always suspected him of a wig," Anne giggled, "or reinforced putees."

With a quick jerking of levers, Armitage stopped the car. He turned around, looked at Sara quietly for a moment and then at Anne. Something in her face told him what he wanted to know.

"Sara," he said, "for a first-class, large gauge sieve, I commend you to any one."

CHAPTER XVI
THE ADVENTURE MATERIALIZES

Sara bowed with mock humility and then raising her head, looked Anne straight in the eyes.

"Miss Wellington, I present Mr. Armitage, an officer—a lieutenant, I think—of the United States Navy."

Anne sat silent for a second and then stretched her hand out over the seat, laughing.

"What a situation!" she exclaimed. "I am pleased to know that my 'Dying Gladiator'—" she paused, and looked inquiringly at Armitage, who had taken and released her hand in silence.

"I don't wish to be impertinent," she continued at length, flushing vividly, "but I feel it is my right to know why you posed as a physical instructor and entered service in our house. Surely I—you—you must have had some good reason."

"Anne," Sara hastened to relieve Armitage of apparent confusion, or irritation, she could not tell which, "naturally his reasons for the deceit were excellent." She looked at her friend with a significant raising of the brows. "I—those reasons still exist, do they not, Jack?" She scowled admonishingly at him.

Armitage, who plainly diagnosed Sara's drift, was smiling broadly, as Anne looked at him with a curious, wondering expression.

"They still exist—decidedly, Sara," he said. He paused for a second, and then continued in the lamest sort of way, "Will you let me be a driver just a little while longer, Miss Wellington? It is really important. When I explain everything you 'll understand. Of course, I 've been governed by the best motives."

Anne was somewhat more dignified.

"Certainly, I have not the slightest objection to having a naval officer for a driver—if you have none. I must say, though, I shall be eager to learn the reasons for your rather—rather unconventional behavior."

"You shall be the first one to know," replied Jack, with quite a different meaning in mind than that which Sara Van Valkenberg read, whose eyes, by the way, were dancing with excitement.

There was an awkward silence for a moment and Jack was turning to the wheel when Anne leaned forward.

"You must tell me about the Navy, sometime," she said. "I have begun to feel I am rather a poor American. Where are you attached?"

"I 'm with the torpedo flotilla at present," said Armitage. "By the way, Miss Wellington, that reminds me of my request for liberty to-night. The boats are going out and—and—it's rather important I go with them. I shall be back before midnight."

"Oh!" Sara's exclamation was so sharp and eager that both Jack and Anne started.

"I have it!" She leaned forward eagerly as both turned to her. "I know. We 'll make him take us out with the boats to-night. Can you imagine anything more thrilling? I have never been on a naval vessel in my life—and they 'll shoot torpedoes. Night attack, Port Arthur, and all that sort of thing, don't you know."

Anne was quite carried away.

"Good! Oh, that would be—" She stopped short as a sudden thought came to her. "Do you suppose—" she said slowly, "that you could, Mr. Armitage? I should love the experience. But perhaps—"

"Nonsense," interrupted Sara. "Of course he can take us. Did n't we see that crowd of women on one of the torpedo boats at the King's Cup race?"

"That boat was not in commission," said Jack. "You might be court-martialled if the commanding officer of the flotilla saw you." He spoke lightly, but running clearly through his mind was the uncompromising phraseology of Article 250 of the Navy Regulations: "Officers commanding fleets, divisions, or ships shall not permit women to reside on board of, or take passage in, any ship of the Navy in commission for sea service." Violation of this meant court-martial and perhaps dismissal from the service. And yet Sara's proposition thrilled him potently. He could not deny his eagerness to do as the young women wished. To have Anne at his side for long hours on a footing of equality! As he looked at her now with her lips parted, her eyes blazing with interest, her cheeks flushed, the penalty of disobeying that odious Article 250 seemed, at worst, slight. Besides, the *D'Estang* was assigned to him for special service to do with her as he saw fit. There might be a loophole there.

Anne, who had been pondering his words, looked up.

"If you are thinking only of us, I should n't mind one bit. I should love dearly to go. I have often seen the torpedo boats from my windows and wished to be on one of them. They look so black and venomous!"

"All right. I'll take you." Armitage looked at them with serious face. "There may be some danger. It is n't yachting, you know."

"Of course it isn't," said Sara.

"Certainly not," echoed Anne. "And besides, Mr. Armitage, I 've never faced real danger in my life—except once when my polo pony ran away. Oh, I want to go!"

"I should like to change my clothes." Armitage glanced humorously at his livery.

"Of course," said Anne. "I tell you; you leave us at Berger's, drive home and change your clothes, then you can pick us up there and we 'll leave the car at O'Neill's until we return. How is that? We will have a lobster ordered for you."

"Don't bother about that, please. I shall have to run over to the island when I come back from The Crags, to prepare the way. Take a taxicab and be at the Navy Landing—no, that would n't be wise; some one might see you. Go to the New York Yacht Club station and I, or Johnson, my second, will be there in the *D'Estang*'s launch. We are the outer boat in the slips and you can come aboard over the stern without any one seeing you. Don't be a minute later than seven-thirty o'clock—that is," he added, "if you are serious about making the trip."

"Serious!" exclaimed Sara.

"Oh, we are serious," said Anne, "and Mr. Armitage—you 're awfully good!"

A tall, grave, young ensign met the two excited girls at the hour designated and shot them across the bay to the torpedo boat slips in silence.

"He 's a nice-looking boy," whispered Sara. "But I wonder,—he does n't seem altogether to approve."

Anne, who had been studying the officer, smiled easily.

"That isn't it; he's embarrassed. For heaven's sake, Sara, don't try to make me feel *de trop* at this stage."

The young man *was* embarrassed; Anne had diagnosed correctly. And it was with great relief that he turned them over to Armitage, who led them to a hatch and thence down a straight iron ladder to the wardroom. Anne watched the precise steward adjusting a centrepiece of flowers upon the mess table and then glanced around the apartment, which was lined with rifles, cutlasses, and revolvers in holsters.

"How interesting, Mr. Armitage," she said. "Do you recall the last time we were in a cabin together?" smiling. "How absurd it was!"

"Wasn't it," laughed Armitage. He left the wardroom and returned in a few minutes with two officers' long, blue overcoats and caps.

"These are your disguises. I'll send an orderly down to take you up to the bridge when we get well under way—"

"Do we really have to wear these?" Sara viewed the overcoats with mock concern.

"Must," laughed Armitage. "It is going to be cold and it looks like rain. I'd tuck my hair up under the caps as much as possible if I were you. Damp salt air is bad for hair."

"You mean you wish us to look like men," asserted Sara.

"I merely want you to be appropriate to the picture."

Sara looked at him mischievously.

"Why not the entire uniform, then?"

"Sara!" cried Anne, as Jack ducked out of the door.

"Anne," Sara placed her hand on Anne's arm, "are you interested in Jack Armitage?"

The girl looked at the dark burning cheeks of the handsome full-blooming young woman in front of her.

"Don't be silly, Sara."

"I'm not silly," said Mrs. Van Valkenberg, half humorously. "I really want to know."

"Why?"

"Why, because if you're not, I want you to keep in the background. For I think I'd—rather like to—enlist in the Navy."

Anne could not tell why, but Sara had succeeded in irritating her.

CHAPTER XVII
THE NIGHT ATTACK

As a smart young seaman escorted the two young women to the bridge and placed them beside the six-pounder gun, the two destroyers, *Jefferson* and *D'Estang* and the torpedo boats *Barclay, Rogers, Bagley, Philip,* and *Dyer* were sweeping between Fort Adams and Rose Island in echelon formation. Long columns of gray-black smoke pouring from the funnels, mingled with the heavy haze of the August evening. There was a bobble of a sea on and as the *Jefferson* signalled for the vessels to come up into line, the scene presented by the grim, but lithe torpedo boats, each hurrying across the waves to its appointed position, rolling in the sea hollows and pitching clouds of spray over grimy bows, appealed suggestively to Miss Wellington, who stood with her hand tightly clenched in Sara's. Huge blue-black clouds, with slivery shafts showing through the rents the wind had made, banked the western horizon, and out to seaward the yellow Brenton Reef light vessel rolled desolate on the surge.

"Is n't it beautiful," murmured Anne, half to herself. "It is so different from being on the *Mayfair*, is n't it?"

"Is n't it beautiful," murmured Anne. "So different from being on the *Mayfair*, is n't it?"

"Is n't it beautiful," murmured Anne. "So different from being on the *Mayfair*, is n't it?"

Sara nodded.

"So much more fun," she replied. "Much more thrilling."

As a matter of fact, the atmosphere of expectancy filled the vessel. Armitage, concerned with the navigation of the ship, his cap reversed to keep the wind from getting under the peak and lifting it into the sea, had neglected them utterly, and the junior had not withdrawn his head from the chart booth for half an hour.

Time and again Jack's face swept past, unseeing them, toward the quartermaster with hands on the wheel, at the rear of the bridge, crying crisply:

"Helm to port."

And the quartermaster replied as he twisted the wheel:

"Helm to port, sir."

Then—

"Ease your helm!"

"Ease your helm, sir."

The dark had fallen now. Ahead the Point Judith acetylene buoy sent its rays toward them. When they came abreast of it, it was pitch black and the white light on Watch Hill was made out to the southeastward. Suddenly from the *Jefferson's* deck a series of red and white lights began to wink and blink. Answering signals twinkled over a mile of water and the boats stopped their engines, rolling like logs on the waters.

Armitage walked over to Anne and Sara, who, in their coats and caps, looked not unlike officers themselves.

"How do you like it?"

"Oh, it is terribly interesting!" said Anne. "What are you going to do now?"

"Wait for the battleships, I imagine," said Armitage. "We don't really torpedo them," he added. "The object is to get as close as possible without being observed. They try to locate us with searchlights. As soon as they see us they put the light on us and fire a red star. After that star is fired the discovered boat must steam full speed for the quarry for one minute and then fire a green star and turn on her lights. The distance from the battleship to the boat is measured and if we are within torpedo range, two thousand yards, the torpedo boat wins. If the distance is greater, we are technically out of action—the battleship wins."

"How interesting!" Anne gazed at Armitage admiringly. "And that is what you would do in real warfare then—rush into the very face of the battleship's firing in the effort to blow her up?"

"About that," smiled Armitage.

"But what a risk! You must steam through a perfect hail of bullets, with chances of striking with your torpedo largely against you. And even if you do strike you are liable to pay the price with your lives. Am I not right?"

"These pirates of the flotilla," laughed Jack, "do not think of the price. They're in the Navy to think of other things."

"And is that the spirit of the American Navy?"

"Of course," Armitage looked at her curiously. "Why not?"

Anne laughed and shrugged her shoulders.

"Oh, I don't know. I know something of the British and French Navies, but patriotism—the sort of spirit you speak of—has always appeared to me such an abstract thing as regards America. It's because, I suppose, I have never known anything about it, because I have been more or less of an expatriate all my life."

Jack had been watching a display of Ardois lights from the *Jefferson's* mast. He turned away, but spoke over his shoulder.

"Don't be that, Miss Wellington, for you have proved to me that a girl or a child, reared as you have been, can be American in every instinct and action. I had never believed that."

He hurried away to the bridge rail and Anne's arm turned red under the impress of Sara's fingers.

In compliance with the *Jefferson's* signals, the engines of the flotilla began to throb and the boats turned to the eastward.

A cry came from the *D'Estang's* lookout. Anne and Sara leaned forward and saw that a blundering sailing vessel—her dark sails a blotch against the sky, her hull invisible—was careening just ahead. She had no lights, and curses on the heads of coastwise skippers who take risks and place other vessels in jeopardy merely to save oil, swept through the flotilla like ether waves.

Armitage let a good Anglo-Saxon objurgation slip from his tongue as he turned toward the yeoman.

"Half speed!"

"Half speed, sir," answered the yeoman as he tugged at the engine room telegraph.

All eyes were now on the schooner. How was she heading? A group of seamen stood beside Armitage and Johnson on the bridge, trying to ascertain that important point. A flash of lightning gave a momentary glance of greasy sails bulged to port.

"She's on the starboard tack, crossing the flotilla!"

"All right." There was relief in Jack's voice as he called for full speed ahead.

"It's no fun to ram a merchantman, with all the law you get into," said the signal quartermaster, standing near the young women. "And if they hit you, good-bye."

But the schooner had a knowing captain. He had no intention of trying to cross all those sharp bows. He quickly tacked between the *D'Estang* and *Barclay* and passed the rest of the boats astern.

Slowly the boats were loafing along now.

At ten-thirty the Jefferson winked her signals at the rest of the flotilla.

"Put out all lights."

As the young women glanced over the sea the truck lights died responsively. Then the green and red starboard and port lamps and lights in wardroom and galley went out and men hurried along the deck placing tarpaulins over the engine room gratings. Only the binnacle lights remained and these were muffled with just a crack for the helmsman to peer through.

A great blackness settled over the waters. To Anne, always an impressionable girl, it was as though all life had suddenly been obliterated from the face of them. Her hand tightened its grasp on Sara's fingers, for as the vessel plunged along there was a palpable impression that the flotilla, now hurrying forward in viewless haste, was pitched for the supreme test. Off to the seaward signal lights from the parent ship *Racine*, having on board the officer in charge of the Navy's mobile defences—which is to say, torpedo boats—had flared and died. The battleships were approaching.

Anne, quivering with excitement, peered out through the night; nothing but darkness. Below, lined along the rails, she caught dull outlines of the white caps of the seamen, all as eager to defeat the battleships as their officers. She saw the phosphorescent gleam from a shattered wave. But she heard nothing, not even the swish of water.

Johnson approached diffidently, and leaned over the rail at their side, straining his eyes into the night.

"The chances of making a successful attack," he said, "are best if we approach from almost ahead, a little on the bow. Then we are lessening the distance between us at the sum of the speeds of the flotilla and the battleships. We'll hit up about twenty-five knots when we see them. Of—"

A low incisive voice sounded forward, a blotch of a hand and arm pointing. There was a movement on the bridge as a dark object came close. It was the *Jefferson*. A dull figure leaned over her bridge with a megaphone.

"We've blown out some boiler tubes and scalded a couple of men, *D'Estang*. Go in ahead."

"All right," Jack's voice was muffled.

Again came the voice of the lookout and the arm pointed ahead.

"Oh!" Anne pinched Sara's arm. "I see them. See those great black shadows over there?" She stepped forward. "Shall I tell them?"

But Armitage had seen. He turned to the yeoman.

"Full speed, ahead!"

"Full speed, ahead, sir."

The slender hull throbbed with the giant pulsings of the two sets of engines. There was not another sound. It was as though the vessel were plunging through an endless void. In the darkness astern arose a spear-like puff of crimson flame. Again it appeared and again, quivering, sinister.

"Damn the *Barclay*; she's torching!" There came a shout from out of the dark and in an instant two great beams of lambent light cut wide swaths through the pall. They were too high; they missed the *D'Estang* altogether and rested on the *Barclay's* smoke, which rose and tumbled and billowed and writhed like a heavy shroud in the ghastly shafts.

"They 've missed us and are trying to get the *Barclay*. Come on!" Jack's voice was vibrant with the joy of the test. He was kneeling on the bridge, a megaphone in his hand. He turned it toward the women. "Crouch down beside that gun and stay down, please, until this is over."

As he spoke, the leading battleship, the dreadnaught *Arizona*, was getting her searchlight beams down, and all unseen, the *D'Estang* and she were approaching each other at a total speed of thirty-seven knots.

Nearer they came and the destroyer was almost to the great dark blur, with the shining arms radiating from her like living tails from a dead comet, when, with terrible suddenness and intensity almost burning, the *Arizona* flashed a sixty-inch searchlight directly down on the destroyer's bridge. Sara stifled a scream and Anne bowed her head to the deck to shut out the fearful blaze. Armitage, standing upright now and rubbing open his eyes, saw that the time had come to turn, and quickly. The *D'Estang* was approaching the battleship, pointing toward her port bow. The idea of the manoeuvre was to turn in a semicircle, passing the *Arizona* at a distance of about two hundred yards. He shouted the order.

"Hard—a—port."

There was an instant's silence and the face of the quartermaster was seen to turn pale in the glare of the relentless searchlight.

"Wheel rope carried away, sir."

Armitage fairly threw himself across the bridge, but Johnson was there first. Quiet, unemotional Johnson, his hat off now, his hair dishevelled, and his eyes blazing.

"The helm is jambed hard a-starboard!" he cried.

In an instant the situation crystallized itself into a flashing picture upon Anne's mind. She had held the wheel on her father's yacht; but it was not that which made her see. It was divination, which fear or danger sometimes brings to highly sensitized minds—just as it brought the same picture to Sara's mind. With helm thus jambed, it meant that the *D'Estang* would have to turn in the same direction in which the *Arizona* was ploughing along at a twelve-knot speed. In making this turn she could not possibly clear, but must strike the battleship. On the other hand she was too near to be stopped in time to avoid going across the bows of that great plunging mass of drab steel, and being cut in two.

Anne, crouching immovable, her eyes fixed on Armitage, saw his head half turn in her direction, then with the automatic movement of a machine, he reached for the port engine room telegraph and with a jerk threw the port engine full speed astern. The bridge quivered as though it were being torn from its place; throughout the hull sounded a great metallic clanking. There came a new motion. The destroyer was spinning like a top, the bow almost at a standstill, the stem swinging in a great arc.

It was like the working out of a problem in dynamics. Nearer they came. Anne could now make out the great shape of the battleship; the dull funnels belching black clouds of smoke, which, merging with the night, were immediately absorbed; the shadowy, basket-like masts, from which the search-light rays went forth; the long, vaguely protruding twelve-inch guns. A whistle, tremulous and piercing, shrilled along the battleship's deck; dull white figures were clambering into the port life boats. Still closer now! Anne could hear the heavy swish of waters under the *Arizona's* bows. Her nerves were tight strung, prepared for the crash of steel against steel and the shock of the submersion. There was no sound from the *Arizona* now. Her bridge had echoed with shouts of warning. The time for that had passed. Armitage had not uttered a sound. Straight he stood by the telegraph, tense and rigid, his hand clutching the lever.

Around came the stern with fearful momentum, so close—but clear of the giant hull—that the gunner's mate at the stern torpedo tube took his chew of tobacco and, as he afterwards put it, "torpedoed the battleship with his eyes shut." Now the stern was pointed directly toward the *Arizona*, hardly five yards away. Armitage, bending over the telegraph, jerked sharply upon the lever, throwing the port engine full speed ahead again. He stood up and glanced quickly astern. Like a live thing, the *D'Estang* jumped clear.

Sara leaned heavily on Anne's shoulder with little tearless sobs. But Anne, crouching in the position she had maintained since the search-light had blinded the bridge, still watched Jack with eyes that seemed to transfix him.

A figure leaped to the end of the battleship's bridge.

"The Admiral's compliments, *D'Estang*!"

The engines were stopped now and Armitage and Johnson and a group of men were working at the helm. Sara raised her head.

"Anne," she said solemnly. "I never wanted to kiss a man until this minute." Mischievously she made a move as though to arise. The girl's hand clenched upon her arm.

"Don't be an idiot," she said. "Can't you see how busy they are? Besides, Sara, no man likes to be kissed by two girls—at the same time."

As Jack, once more a chauffeur, drove under the *porte cochère* at The Crags, shortly before one o'clock, Anne sat for a moment in her seat after her friend had alighted. Sara looked back with a little smile and then walked toward the door, which a footman had opened.

"Mr. Armitage," said Anne in a low voice, "I want to thank you for many things to-night—for one thing above all. I cannot tell you what it is, for I hardly know myself." She paused, and Jack, who was toying with the switch lever, looked at her curiously. "It's a new viewpoint, I fancy. Somehow—I have a feeling that there is more to this country, my country, than Fifth Avenue, Central Park, Tuxedo, Long Island, and Newport—something bigger and finer than railroads. I am glad to feel that, and I thank you."

CHAPTER XVIII
ANNE WELLINGTON HAS HER FIRST TEST

Sara was waiting for Anne in the hall. She had taken off her hat and stood idly swinging it. A single globe was lighted in the chandelier overhead and the extremities of the great apartment were lost in gloom.

"Well, dear," Sara yawned broadly, "I fancy we shall sleep to-night."

Anne had thrown her arm over Sara's shoulders and they were walking toward the stairs when Koltsoff appeared from the shadow, confronting them.

"Oh! Prince Koltsoff! How you frightened me," said Anne in a low voice, drawing back.

"A thousand pardons. It would have grieved me had I thought of doing that."

Sara observed him with irritation. There was, however, so much of the exotic about the man, as to render him attractive, even to her. Tall, well—if slimly—built; in manner graceful—"silken" was the designation that occurred to her—there could be no question as to the potency of his personality: a potency, by the way, from whose spell, she had learned in various ways throughout the evening, Anne was not entirely aloof. It was perfectly clear to Sara, that with Armitage, strong and clever in a wholesome masculine way, Anne was the light-hearted, mischievous, pure-minded girl—his ideal of American young womanhood. But now she caught the other note of her character—an untrue note, but none the less positive—and the other look in her eyes. Her voice was deeper, more womanly, more surcharged with underlying things, as she spoke to the Russian, and Sara could see she was breathing more rapidly.

"I have been waiting to see you, Miss Wellington," he was saying. "I have waited so long." There was a note of pathos in his voice.

"Is it important—now?" asked Anne, and her friend tugged at her sleeve. "I am very tired and sleepy."

"For a few moments, that is all," persisted the Prince gently. "Is it too much?"

Sara, inwardly raging, detected the subtle appeal which this man, so versed apparently in the emotions of womanhood, was making to the inherent maternal, protective, sympathetic instincts of the girl, who, now they were aroused, was smiling patiently.

"Very well, Prince Koltsoff. Don't bother to wait, Sara. Good-night."

"Such a day of weariness, Miss Wellington,", said the Prince, as he followed Anne to a bench running along the foot of the staircase. "One of my men,—calf-head,—was arrested in Boston."

"Arrested! Really! What had he been doing?"

"Nothing, I assure you, save trying to leave this bestial country. He had been of service to me in Newport and elsewhere. I was worried. I am worried. He was allowed to go. But they took valuable papers concerning Austria from him. How can I get them? Am I undone?" Koltsoff raised his eyes. "How can I say? Steinberg at Boston is in Maine. And so—" Koltsoff tossed his hand in the air—"I have spent," he at last continued, "more than twenty thousand roubles on the matter. I have spent five thousand roubles on the dumbhead, Yeasky, who has not the brains or courage of a mouse. I am discouraged." He caught her hand, pressed it to his forehead, and released it. "But I oppress you with my diplomatic cares," he murmured. "It has been the first time I ever burdened a woman with them. You—you are different, because you are of the few gifted to bear, to solve them."

Anne made no reply.

"You hold safely that which I placed in your keeping?" he asked after a pause.

His hand felt its way to hers, lying inert on the cushion, his fingers closing softly upon it. She did not withdraw it, but lowered her head.

"Was it in connection with that your man was arrested in Boston?"

Koltsoff laughed.

"They thought to connect him with it. But—" he pressed Anne's fingers, "the connecting link happened to be in your—jewelry safe."

Anne, thrilled at the part she was playing in the mysterious diplomatic episode, laughed softly. Somehow it all appeared bigger even than dodging under battleships' bows,—certainly more subtle. Koltsoff gazed at her admiringly.

"My dear Miss Wellington," he said, "do you realize more and more, that of which I spoke to-day—your fitness for the international sphere? Your beauty—your coolness—the temper of your spirit—your ability to sway strong men, as you have swayed me—do you appreciate all? Are you proud that you have swayed me?"

"Prince Koltsoff!" Anne's voice rang with doubt and anguish and yet—pride.

She was tired and spent with the day and as his arm stole, almost snake-like, about her waist, she raised a nerveless hand, plucked feebly to remove the fingers pressing into her side, and then let her hand fall to the cushion.

His head was bending over her, his face was very close. Some vivid instinct told her that he must not kiss her. She tried to struggle but she could not. The next instant she was living that epoch which innocence may only know ere it perishes—a man's lips making free with eyes and mouth and cheeks. She lay now, half in his arms, looking at him with wide, startled eyes, her lips parched.

"Anne," he bent forward to kiss her again, but she turned her head away and then, again, her unchanging eyes sought his face. "What I have done—what I have meant, I shall make clear to your parents to-morrow. To you I can say nothing now. You—ah, of course know the European custom."

"Please let me go." There was a tired sob in Anne's voice.

"But I have not yet told you that which I wish to say." Anne tore from his arm and started up.

"You haven't! Oh, very well. I am listening."

"You were out with the torpedo boats tonight. You were upon the boat with Lieutenant Armitage."

"I—" Anne paused. Armitage, without attempting to obtain promises of secrecy as to the mission of the flotilla, had pointed out that all information of the sort was absolutely confidential and that above all the ability of a torpedo boat destroyer to get within two hundred yards of a battleship was not news that the Government would care to have disseminated, even though it were the exception rather than the rule. This thought shot through Anne's mind.

"You quite surprise me," she said finally.

"Oh, I really do not," smiled Koltsoff. "As I have informed you, we diplomats are omnipresent. Therefore I do not surprise you when I say that you and your friend were on the *D'Estang*; that the *Jefferson* had an accident and sent two scalded men to the hospital. All that—pouf!" Koltsoff snapped his fingers. "That is immaterial—who cares about such manoeuvres as the Navy of the United States indulge in! But," and Koltsoff bent toward her with unwinking eyes, "this is important: the *D'Estang* became separated from the rest of the fleet and there are reports that she discharged a new sort of torpedo at the battleship. That is interesting—

important to me. I feared I could not ascertain until I learned that my skilled coadjutor, my fellow diplomat," he nodded at her, "was present on the *D'Estang*."

"Why do you ask me? Why don't you apply to Mr. Armitage?"

"Ah, he would tell me, of course!" laughed Koltsoff sarcastically. "In any event, I have yet to know him. He was at Washington when I arrived in Newport, and since his return has been at the Torpedo Station but one night. My men have not been able to find him."

Anne had forgotten her weariness now.

"There seems to be something, at least, in the American Navy that you find worthy of close interest," she said.

An expression of indifference settled upon the Prince's face.

"Ah, if you know of the Navy, you know the nations are always interested in the new devices and plans of other nations. I once paid fifteen thousand roubles for the plans of an English fort."

"And so diplomacy is stealing or buying information, then?"

"Diplomacy is anything, Anne."

"You interest me, Prince Koltsoff."

"But the *D'Estang*—I imagine she was not successful with her torpedoing." Inwardly he was cursing Yeasky, as he had been all the evening; Yeasky had never missed a trip of the *D'Estang*.

Anne, beginning to see, had worked into her cool, malicious mood.

"You must not be so imaginative," she gaped [Transcriber's note: gasped?]. "And now if you'll excuse me—it's two o'clock."

"But Anne—Miss Wellington!" The Prince was at her side. "You do not really intend to deny me!" He shook his head, as though dazed. "It cannot be possible that our understanding is so incomplete. I had dared to hope, to believe that our interests were so swiftly merging. And what is it that I ask! Merely a slight question about the *D'Estang*. Anne—is it upon so little a thing that you fail me? Would that you might try *me* with a bigger, greater test. You should see!"

"Do you mean that, really?"

"As God is my judge!" cried the Prince fervently.

"Then," said Anne seriously, "say good-night to me. Pardon me, but I am tired."

"But the *D'Estang*," cried Koltsoff insistently. "My plans—my life—"

"What!" interrupted Anne, as a thought was born of his words. "I understood that this was merely a matter of routine naval intelligence."

Koltsoff mopped his forehead.

"That is true," he hastened to say, "but matters of routine are the greater part of the lives of such as we. Our success depends upon it, alone. Pardon me, but I must insist that you tell me what I have asked." He had almost backed her against the wainscoting.

"And I won't tell you, Prince Koltsoff."

"Why not, pray?"

"I will tell you why," her voice quivered with emotion. "This morning you convinced me pretty thoroughly that I had no right to call myself an American. I still feel that way, don't you know. But to-night I 've seen brave and devoted men risking their lives and perfecting themselves in their calling not only through professional interest but through love of their country and their flag, and dare-devil enthusiasm in serving under a flag that means so much to them. The father of the junior officer on the *D'Estang* is a farmer and the captain of the *Barclay* is the son of an insurance clerk. But they're all of one cut and out of one mould—American fighting men who would shoot or knock down any one who dared utter in their presence such words as I have listened to from you—more shame to me—without a single emotion, save amusement." She ran on breathlessly, "Whatever happened on the *D'Estang* to-night, important or unimportant, is the concern of the Navy of my country alone. Hereafter, in anything you say or do, Prince Koltsoff, remember I am learning to be an American—" she stopped and smiled at her own ardor, "so please don't say anything to discourage me."

Koltsoff, who had been listening in silence, without making a movement, suddenly bowed his head.

"I am sorry, Miss Wellington!" His voice was broken and sincerely so. "I misunderstood!" He sank to one knee and seized the bottom of her skirt.

"Don't, Prince Koltsoff, please!" Anne was swiftly relenting. She drew her skirt away and the Prince arising took her hand.

"Ah, please!" she said.

"Not until I hear you are not angry."

"I am not angry."

He had drawn her close to him and they were looking into each other's eyes.

"What is it?" she asked weakly. Her very personality seemed ebbing from her.

"You love me?" His voice was almost a whisper.

She smiled wanly.

"*Is* this love?"

"Is it! What is love? Love is giving—yielding. Love knows neither country nor patriotism nor religion!" His glittering eyes were still holding hers. "And so," his voice was low but masterful, "I ask you—not that I care vitally for the answer of itself; you must know, must understand my motives—I ask you, did the *D'Estang* discharge a torpedo to-night?"

Long they looked at each other and then slowly the girl shook her head.

"You mean no? She did not?" Koltsoff's voice was eager, his arms tightened about her.

"I do not mean anything."

Then suddenly she twisted out of his arms and stood with white face and parted lips, pointing to the stairway.

"Now," she cried, "go! Go, I tell you," she stamped her foot as Koltsoff hesitated. "Go, or I shall hate you!"

CHAPTER XIX
AN ENCOUNTER IN THE DARK

While Anne was detained below by Koltsoff, Sara had gone to her room. She lay awake for a long time and when her maid informed her that Emilia was still waiting for her mistress, she gave up the idea of seeing her and went to sleep.

Armitage in the meantime had placed the car in the garage, entered the house by the servants' door, and was now sitting in his stocking feet, smoking a pipe, waiting for quiet to fall upon the house. His nerves were still taut with the events of the evening; his mind very much awake and alert. He thrilled with the thought that in all probability he would have a commendatory letter from the Admiral to send to his father and that a duplicate would be published to the fleet. As for his position in the house, that was hourly growing more precarious. So far as he could gather, almost every one but the Prince and the Wellington boys knew his identity, and it certainly could not be long before this ignorant minority would be wiped out. There must be action, and quick action. With the Prince away for the night the opportunity could never be better. He was bent now on taking advantage of it.

It was nearly three o'clock when he left his room, walked along the heavily carpeted hall, and descended the stairs in the front of the house to the second floor. The dim light was flowing from the hall below but no lamps were lighted above. He turned, crouching, and made his way along toward Koltsoff's rooms. Footsteps sounded on the stairs and as he flattened himself against the wall the skirts of a woman fluttered past him. A second later the door of Miss Wellington's rooms opened and in the light rushing forth, he saw Anne enter. She was weeping. He heard the exclamation of the maid and Anne saying something in reply. Then the door closed.

For five minutes Armitage remained immovable. Then taking from his pocket a skeleton key and a long thin roll of wire he crept to Koltsoff's door, which he had marked in the afternoon. As he placed his hand on the knob it turned in his grasp and opened. There was a single electric bulb, burning in a crimson globe, and although Armitage had time to jump back, the light flowing from the open door fell full upon him. He stood breathing quickly, watching the newcomer, his forearm poised along his waist, the fist doubled. Without a word, the man slowly closed the door. As Armitage waited an electric dark-light flashed in his face with blinding suddenness. Then it went out.

"Not now," came a whispered voice, "Prince Koltsoff has returned. He has but gone into his room."

Jack did not reply. His hand shot into his pocket and came out with a dark-light similar to that which had been used against him. As he aimed the instrument and pressed the spring a brown seamed face with a head of heavy dark hair appeared in the centre of the illumination.

"Let us have done with lights; they are not necessary," said the man. The voice was cultivated, the manner gentle. "And besides, they are not safe."

"What do you want?" Armitage's voice rose with an impatient inflection.

"I might ask that of you," was the soft reply. "But come, a fair exchange, you know, since our quarry seems to be the same. Although passing as Prince Koltsoff's secretary, in reality I am Turnecki, of the Austrian State Department. You are of the secret service of this country."

Jack was cautious.

"I am a burglar, if you must know," he said. "And if you make any outcry, I'll kill you."

"Oh, no you are not," smiled the man, shaking his head.

Without a word Armitage leaned forward and seized the man by the arm.

"Come to my room with me," he said.

There was great dignity in the man's voice as he placed his hand admonishingly upon Jack's arm.

"Don't do that. I am quite ready to go with you."

But Jack's fingers closed more tightly.

"I am glad you feel that way," he said grimly, "because I want to talk to you. However, I think I'll make sure. Come on."

At the stairs he gently pushed the man ahead of him and followed him to his door. He switched on the light and then, mindful of the watchman on the grounds below, threw a heavy towel over the globe.

"Now, Herr Turnecki, or Koltsoff's secretary, or anything you please to call yourself," he said indicating a chair,—he himself stood at the bureau filling his pipe,—"tell me what I can do for you."

The man bowed, and for a moment they gazed at each other. Armitage could not dismiss an impression of suspicion concerning him, but aside from something familiar in face and figure and in some of the tones of his voice, he was unable to place him. The putative Austrian seemed to read Jack's thoughts.

"Let me first prove," he said at length, "that I am friendly to you—and perhaps to your interests. I recognized you this morning as an American naval officer I had met two years ago in Vienna. It is my business not to forget faces. You must be aware that I have not informed my—" he grimaced—"master of your identity."

"That is true," said Armitage ruefully. "As a detective I appear to be about as much of a success as a farmer at the helm of a battleship."

"Ah, well," observed the other, "it is a business." He looked at Armitage closely. "I admire the United States. Can I be of service?"

"Perhaps," said Armitage, "but you spoke of similar interests. What can I do for you?"

"Nothing, I fear," said the Austrian. "You must know that recently this man Koltsoff purchased, in some way, the mobilization plans of our army on our northeastern, that is, the Russian frontier. Possession of these by Russia will seriously affect the attitude of our chief, Baron Aehrenthal, toward the State Department at St. Petersburg. So close was the espionage, in which I have played no small part, that he was unable to get them out of his hands before his vessel sailed for New York from Fiume. I fear now, however, that such is not the case."

"You mean he has mailed or expressed them?" asked Jack.

The man shook his head.

"Such things are never transmitted in that way."

Jack's heart bounded with relief.

"Well, would n't that be a reason for attempting it?"

"I should be happy to know that the plans were on their way to the post office in St. Petersburg," shrugging his shoulders. "They would soon be on their return journey—and not by mail."

"Oh," cried Armitage, suddenly remembering his conversation with Thornton. "I think I can put you in the way of recovering your stolen plans." Thereupon he told of the capture of Yeasky and of the papers taken from him, already in the keeping of the secret service men in Boston.

As he spoke Turnecki leaned forward, his eyes blazing, uttering subdued German exclamations. When Armitage had concluded he sprang forward and seized Jack by the hand and then after the manner of his country, kissed him on the cheek.

"A thousand thanks!" he cried. "My servitude ends now; for when Koltsoff awakens I shall be *en route* for Boston. You said that you would send on an order for their delivery."

"Yes, I'll write that now—and then I'll tell you what you can do for me. Of course, you understand that the secret service chaps will require the Austrian Consul to vouch for you."

"Oh, I understand that, of course," said the man.

"All right." Armitage took his fountain pen from his coat lying on the bed and leaned across the bureau, about to write, when he abruptly laid the pen down and half closed his eyes. Some new thought seemed filling his mind and moving him deeply.

"Just a second," he said at length. He walked across the room, jerked the towel from the lamp, gazed closely at the man for an instant, and then with an exclamation continued to the door, which he locked, placing the key in his pocket. Returning he stood directly in front of the man, who had arisen.

"Well," he said, "of all fools, commend me! How do you feel, Yeasky, with your beard off and wig on; your German dialect and your painted scar?"

The man looked at Armitage with face utterly expressionless.

"You are mistaken," he said.

"Am I?" sneered Jack. "I have been mistaken so far as you are concerned several times in the past." He laughed grimly. "But not this time, old boy. Come, pass out that control."

"I have n't it."

"You lie. Take off your coat."

Yeasky deliberately divested himself of his coat and threw it at Jack's feet. Then he slapped all his pockets.

"You see," he said, "I have not got it."

"Who has?"

"Koltsoff, I suppose. He did not speak of it to me."

"What did he speak of? What are you here for? You were released upon condition that you leave this country. I suppose you know I can put you in the way of spending several years in an American jail."

"I had intended going, but I received his orders and had to come to him. So I escaped from the steamship, and returned to Newport."

"Did you want to come?"

"No, I am sick of the service. It is all work and danger and no credit. He receives it all."

"Then why did you obey his orders?"

Yeasky raised his shoulders and smiled significantly.

"Siberia," he said. "The arms of such as Koltsoff are very long in cases of those who fail them."

"What did Koltsoff want you here for?"

"To confer with me. He thought we would be safe from spies here. When I saw you I hoped to get an order for the return of the Austrian plans."

"Ump! You nearly succeeded. Did you tell Koltsoff I suspected him?"

"No, that would have made my work appear even more bungling. Listen," added the man earnestly, "I told him I thought my capture had been due to the Austrians, whose system of espionage is really wonderful. That is God's truth," raising his hand solemnly. "I should have believed it myself had I not known you knew."

"If that is true you have done me rather a good turn," said Armitage watching his face closely.

Yeasky drew from his breast a silver ichon.

"It is true." He knelt. "I swear it by this."

"A man's oath is no better than his deeds," replied Armitage musingly. "Look here, Yeasky," he added presently. "I tell you what I am going to do. I am going to turn you over to Chief Roberts of the Newport police and he will hold you for two or three days under an assumed name on the charge of burglary. No one but the watchman and the police and myself will know of your arrest. When I recover the control you will be released, free to stay in this country or go where you please. The only condition is that you attempt in no way to communicate with Koltsoff."

The man bowed his head thoughtfully.

"Besides," resumed Armitage, "I don't know how the secret service people feel about the Austrian plans. I imagine Koltsoff has been making representations to the State Department, and since this Government has no business with them, they may hand them over. If I can help you there, I shall do so. Now," he concluded, "there is the proposition; take it or leave it."

"I'll take it!" replied Yeasky. "As for the Austrian plans, you need not bother about them. You have promised me freedom after two or three days if I keep silent. That is all I ask. Ever since I have been in this country I have been on the point of making up my mind to become a citizen. The Russian Government cannot touch me here, can it?"

"Not unless you have committed a crime."

"I have committed many crimes; none, however, against the Russian Government. I am weary of Koltsoff, weary of this service, weary of this life. There is much money for me here in the practice of my profession."

"You 've already worked in this country, have n't you. Your letter of recommendation from the Eastern Electric—"

"Was forged," said Yeasky quietly. "No, I have never been employed here. I came from Fiume with Prince Koltsoff. I had some thought at the time of deserting; but I was afraid. Now my mind is made up. I want to remain here; I shall remain. I have a brother in Chicago."

"Good," said Armitage. "Come on, now, quickly."

Softly they went down the stairs, and after switching off the burglar alarm, Jack escorted the man out of the servants' door, where he whistled softly. The watchman came up on the run.

"Here's a burglar I caught," said Jack cheerfully. "He was lurking in the second floor hallway."

The watchman, a former New York policeman, was not excited.

"All right," he said. "We 'll take him to the gate house and telephone for the patrol."

This was done and within half an hour the sidelights of the heavy vehicle plunged out of the darkness to the gate.

"Now, don't worry," whispered Armitage, as the man was bundled into the wagon. "I 'll have the chief on the 'phone within five minutes. Remember your part."

Yeasky nodded, and the wagon rumbled away.

It was a very angry chief that Jack, sitting in the butler's hallway, got on the 'phone. But within a few minutes he was laughing and promising to obey Armitage's wishes in every respect.

The clock was striking four when Armitage arose from the telephone. He stood, stretching himself and yawning for a moment, and then stole to the stairs.

"I have spent eventful days before this," he smiled, "but this one breaks all records." As he slipped past the door of Anne's suite, he stopped just an instant.

"Good-night, Anne," he said.

CHAPTER XX
WITH REFERENCE TO THE DOT

Armitage gained next morning a very perfect idea of the regard which the Wellington household held for the head of it. Mr. Wellington had waited in New York for the *Mayfair*, and not only Anne, but Mrs. Wellington and the boys took their post on the southeastern veranda soon after nine o'clock, while Ronald glued his eyes to the big telescope. After he had alternately picked up a white Lackawanna tug and a Maine-bound steamship as the *Mayfair*, Anne lost patience.

"Mother," she said, "why not send for McCall? He used to be a sailor, I believe, and will, no doubt, be able to pick up the yacht miles farther away than we can."

Something resembling a smile crossed the mother's face.

"Very well, Anne; send for him."

A footman was summoned and within a few minutes Armitage was the centre of an interested group. He swept the Narragansett shore for a few minutes and then turned to Mrs. Wellington.

"There's a large white yacht with a yellow funnel, which has a silver band on top, this side of Point Judith," he said. "I can see the red glint of her house flag."

"Why, that's the *Mayfair*!" cried Anne. "Come on, mother, Sara."

"She won't be up for three-quarters of an hour, Anne," said her mother.

"I don't care. Come, Sara, we'll raise the flags on the landing ourselves."

As Sara and Anne and the two boys trouped down the path to the cleft in the cliffs, Mrs. Wellington nodded at Jack.

"Quinn reports that you captured a burglar last night, McCall."

Jack smiled.

"Yes, Mrs. Wellington. I caught him in the hall on the second floor. I had him before he could lift a hand and turned him over to the watchman."

"I am indebted to you. What were you doing on the second floor at that hour?"

"I could n't sleep and was smoking in my room when I heard some one pass my door. I went out and saw him flashing a dark lantern below. My shoes were off and I had him before he heard me."

"That was really clever of you. Chief Roberts has informed me that he is a professional, wanted on several other charges. When he sends word I want you to press the charge for me. Of course this will not appear in the newspapers, so please say nothing to any one about it."

As Armitage nodded, she looked at him closely.

"How long do you intend to stay with us, McCall?"

Armitage started.

"Why—I—I—" he paused.

"Oh, no matter. I thought, perhaps, you might be ambitious to join the police force. I think I could help you."

Jack, inwardly raging, flushed and glanced at her uncertainly.

"Thank you," he said, "I 'll consider—I—I 'll let you know."

"Hang her," he said to himself as he walked toward the garage. "Deliver me from an old woman who thinks she has a sense of humor."

Ronald Wellington was a man past fifty, a man whose stature was as large as his mind. He had a shock of gray hair; brilliant hazel eyes like Anne's, but overshadowed by shaggy brows; high cheek bones, and straight lips hidden by a heavy gray mustache. It was said of him that his clothing was only pressed when new and that he purchased a new hat only under the combined pressure of his wife and daughter. He had an immense voice which could be gruff or pleasing, as he willed; in all, a big, strong, wholesome personality, unconventional, but in no sense unrefined. He was in striking contrast to his dapper crony, Robert Marie, who accompanied him from the yacht, a man whose distinction lay in his family, his courtly manners of the old school, and his connoisseurship of wines.

Mrs. Wellington waited on the veranda, but Anne, her brothers, and Sara were at the landing as the gangway of the yacht was lowered. Ronald Wellington seized Anne by the elbows, an old trick of his, and as she stiffened them he lifted her to his face and kissed her. Ronald he slapped on the back, and as for the more sturdy little Royal, he lifted him high in the air and placed him on his shoulder, smiling and nodding pleasantly to Sara. Sara waited for Robert Marie, and thus the party walked to the house. Mrs. Wellington advanced to the rail, smiling, and her husband, setting Royal on the ground, reached up, seized her hands, and drew her face down to his.

"Well, girl," he said, "glad to see me?"

She withdrew her lips and as Sara looked at her, with perhaps a little pathos in her eyes, she saw, spreading over her face that expression, the beauty and charm and inspiration of which are ever the same, in youth and in age, in the countenances of those in whom love still abides unchanging.

They sat on the porch for a few minutes and then, having breakfasted on the *Mayfair*, Mr. Wellington went to his study off the library, where Mrs. Wellington joined him.

"Well, Ronald," she said, "Prince Koltsoff is here."

"Yes," he said, "so you—and the newspapers have told me. What is he—another Ivan?"

"Not in any way. He and Anne seem to be getting on finely."

Mr. Wellington looked at her.

"My mind was so filled with that Northern Atlantic matter last month when you talked of your prince," he said, "that I don't think I did the question justice. It was too far off—and the railroad mess was so confoundedly near. Now then, let's have it."

"How—what do you mean?" asked Mrs. Wellington, a bit uneasily.

"What have you been trying to do, Belle?"

"Why, I have n't been trying to do anything. The situation has shaped itself without any effort on my part."

"You mean Anne loves the Russian! Bosh! How long has he been here—this is the third day!" The room rang with his laughter.

"I did not say that she loved him. I said they seemed to be getting on."

Mr. Wellington clasped his big hands over his knees and gazed at the floor. "Belle," he said, after a few minutes, "the idea of Anne living away off in a foreign country does n't swallow easily. Life is too short—and, Belle, I don't think you have ever loved Anne quite as I have."

Mrs. Wellington thought for a moment of the adoration which this big man had always held for their daughter—an emotion in no way conflicting with his conjugal devotion and yet equally tremendous, and smiled without a trace of jealousy.

"Yes, I think that is true," she said. "Yet of course you cannot question my love for her. I certainly would be the last to thwart her ambitions."

"Nor I," returned Wellington with a sigh. "And yet, Belle, so far as you are concerned, you don't need such a match. Your position certainly needs no assurance, either here or abroad. We are not in the business of buying foreign titles, you know. We don't have to. Besides, we thrashed all that out when Anne was a child. The girl must marry, of course; for years that has hung over me like a bad dream. But it's natural and right and for the best. But, Belle, since she has grown up and her marriage has become a question of narrowing time—especially since that French nobleman, De Joinville, was buzzing around last year—I have had an ambition for grandchildren that can say 'grandpa' in a language I understand. That is the way I feel about it."

His wife laughed at this characteristic speech and reaching out, patted his hand. He, in turn, seized and held her hand, quite covering it.

"Naturally, Ronald, I feel just as you do about having to purchase foreign titles. But it has pleased me to have the Prince here, in view of the fact that several others wanted him. It's akin to the satisfaction you feel, I imagine, when you suddenly appear before the public as owner of the controlling interest in a competitor's railroad."

"I understand," he replied, and gazed at his wife admiringly. "If I had been as good a railroad man as you are a social diplomat, I should be the only railroad man in the country." He laughed his hearty laugh and then glanced at her seriously. "Well, what about Anne?" he asked.

Mrs. Wellington was about to reply when her secretary entered.

"Prince Koltsoff is in the library waiting to pay his respects," said the young woman. "He seemed a little impatient and I told him I would tell you."

"Oh," said Mr. Wellington, as an expression of annoyance crossed his wife's face, "let him come right in."

As he towered over the Prince, seizing his hand with a grip that made the latter wince, Mrs. Wellington could not help noticing a veiled expression of contempt in the nobleman's face. She was aware that to him, her husband represented, of course, the highest plane of existence that Americans attain to, and she could see that the things in him, the things he stood for and had done, which would impress the average American or perhaps the Englishman, carried no appeal to this Russian. To him, she read, Ronald Wellington, in his great, bagging, ill-fitting clothes, was merely an embodiment of the American pig, whose only title to consideration was the daughter he had to give, and his only warrant of respect, his wealth.

"Sit down, Koltsoff," said her husband heartily, but studying him keenly from under his shaggy brows.

"Thank you," replied the Prince, seating himself luxuriously in a great leather chair. "As you must know, Mr. Wellington," he said, at the same time inclining his head toward Mrs. Wellington, "time presses for men in my sphere of life—the diplomatic; that is why I felt I must speak to you at once."

"Certainly," said Mr. Wellington, glancing at his wife, "fire away."

"Your daughter," began the Prince, "I am deeply interested in her. I—" he stopped and smiled.

Mr. Wellington nodded.

"Go on," he said gruffly, now.

"I—I believe I love her."

"You believe?"

"In fact, I do love her. It is about that I wish to speak to you—as to the dower. Naturally the sum you would propose—"

"Wait just a second. Not so fast," said Mr. Wellington. "Does my daughter love—wish to marry you?"

"I have reason to believe she loves me,"—Koltsoff shrugged his shoulders,—"excellent reasons. As to marriage—of course I have no doubt as to her wishes. But first, I must, of course, reach an understanding with you."

"How do you mean?" asked Mr. Wellington, bending forward and impaling the Prince with his eyes. "Did Anne tell you how much she would be willing to have me pay for you?"

"Certainly not," snapped Koltsoff.

"Well, then, listen, Prince Koltsoff. You are here now as our guest and we hope to make your sojourn quite pleasant. But," he took a cigar from a box, lighted it, and thrust the box across the table to Koltsoff. "But we might as well have a clear understanding. It will be better in every way. I have felt that Americans have been altogether too willing to subscribe to European customs in marrying off their daughters. I am going to establish a new precedent, if I can. Am I clear?"

"What do you mean?" Koltsoff's voice quivered with rising indignation. Mrs. Wellington could not have analyzed her emotions had she tried. All she could do was to sit and watch the tottering of the structure she had reared, under the blows of one who had never before interfered in her plans, but whose word was her law.

"I mean that I am unwilling to pay a single red penny for you, or any one else to marry my daughter. If she 's worth anything, she's worth everything. I 'll inform you, however, that she has some money in her own right—not enough to rehabilitate a run-down European estate, but enough to keep the wolf from the door, and, of course, when I get through with it, she 'll share in my estate, which is not inconsiderable."

"But Prince Koltsoff is a man of wealth," said Mrs. Wellington quietly. "He is not of the broken-down sort."

"Oh, I know all about that," said her husband. "All the more reason why this precedent I am trying to establish should find favor in his eyes."

The Prince rose.

"I understand you to say that you refuse the dower rights which any European must, of course, expect?"

"You do, absolutely. If Anne loves you and wants to marry you, that is her right. She is of age. But no dower. Not a cent."

"And you *love* your daughter!" Koltsoff's voice was withering.

Mr. Wellington arose quickly.

"That," he said, "we won't discuss."

"Very well," Koltsoff's voice arose almost to a shriek. "But listen, I do love Anne Wellington and I think she loves me. And with dower or without it, I 'll marry her. And—and—" he clutched at his throat, "you have heard me. I have spoken. I say no more." And he slammed out of the room.

CHAPTER XXI
PLAIN SAILOR TALK

Miss Hatch had some inkling of the Prince's intention when she ushered him into the Wellington study, and as she met Sara in the hall on the way out of the library, she held a gloomy countenance.

"Mrs. Van Valkenberg," she said in response to Sara's bright smile of greeting, "please don't think me impertinent, but—will you, if possible, see that the Prince is not alone with Miss Wellington to-day? And—cannot you prod that terribly sluggish McCall?"

Sara looked at the young woman wonderingly for a minute and then held out her hand, laughing.

"Miss Hatch, you 're a jewel."

Sara found Jack near the garage. But she did not have much success with him. He was grumpy and, replying to Sara's assertion that the situation was rapidly becoming rife with disagreeable possibilities, he replied that he did not care a very little bit, and that Anne could marry all the princes in Christendom for all he cared. So Sara, flushing with impatience, told him he was an idiot and that she would like to shake him. The only satisfaction she derived from the incident was that Anne, who came upon them as they were parting, was grumpy, too. Synchronous moods in the two persons whose interests she held so closely to heart was a symptom, she told herself, that gave warrant for hope.

Rimini had turned up with the new car and in it Anne, Sara, Koltsoff, and Robert Marie went to the Casino. Mrs. Wellington drove to market in her carriage. Mr. Wellington remained in his study and among other things had Buffalo on the telephone for half an hour. Armitage spent the morning with the boys and showed them several shifty boxing and wrestling tricks which won Ronald to him quite as effectually as the jiu-jitsu grip had won his younger brother the preceding day.

At luncheon, Anne's peevish mood had not diminished, which, to Sara, would have been a source of joy had she not feared that it was due to the fact that Koltsoff had not been good company all the morning. He was, in truth, quite at his wits' end to account for the behavior of Yeasky, who had been instructed to get into communication with him by ten o'clock, and had failed to do so. Thus Koltsoff, even when with Anne, had been preoccupied and in need of a great deal of entertaining.

Armitage took him to the city after lunch and as usual was instructed to return to The Crags. This gave Jack opportunity to see Chief Roberts and to learn that Yeasky was resting easily and cheerfully, apparently eager to live up to the very letter of his contract.

Anne was in her room when he returned and Sara was with her. Koltsoff came back in a taxicab in a frightful state of mind, bordering on mental disintegration, about four o'clock—just in time to keep an appointment with his host and Marie to drive to the Reading Room. As he crossed the veranda, a French bull pup ran playfully between his feet and nearly tripped him. He kicked at the animal, which fled squealing down the steps.

"Hey, you," cried the peppery Ronald, "that's my dog."

The Prince turned with a half snarl and flung himself into the house.

"The great big Turk!" said Ronald, turning to Armitage. "What does he want here, anyway?"

It was nearly five o'clock when the telephone of the garage rang and Armitage was ordered to bring Anne's car to the house. Her manner was quiet, her voice very low, as she gave him his orders.

"To town by the back road," she said. She stopped at one or two stores along Thames Street and finally settling herself back in her seat, said, "Now you can drive home."

Armitage looked at her for a second.

"Do you mind if I take a roundabout way? I should like to talk to you."

Anne returned his gaze without speaking.

Then she nodded slowly.

"Yes, if you like," she said.

"Thank you."

He drove the car up the steep side streets, across Bellevue Avenue, and then headed into a little lane. Here he stopped. Overhead ash and beech and maple trees formed a continuous arch. Gray stone walls hedged either side. Beyond each line of wall, pleasant orchards stretched away. The sidewalks were velvet grass. Birds of brilliant plumage flashed among the foliage and their twittering cries were the only sounds. Patches of gold sunlight lay under the orchard trees, level rays flowed heavily through the branches and rested on the moss-grown stones.

The pastoral beauty, the great serenity, the utter peace seemed to preclude words. And the spell was immediately upon the two. The down-turned brim of her hat shaded her eyes, but permitted sunlight to lie upon her mouth and chin and to rest where her hair rippled and flowed about her bare neck.

She raised her face—and her eyes, even, level, wondering, sought his. His eyes were the first to fall, but in them she knew what she had read. Now the sunlight had fallen so low that it lay on her like a garment of light—she seemed some daughter of Hesperus, glorified. The waning afternoon had grown cooler and several blue-white clouds went careening overhead. She looked at them.

"How beautiful!" she said. Then she looked at him again with her steady eyes. "You wished to talk, you said."

Jack nodded.

"Yes, I wish to, but I—I don't know exactly how to say it."

She was smiling now. "How may I help you?"

He shook his head doggedly.

"I am a sailor, Miss Wellington."

"You mean I am to hear plain sailor talk?" she quoted. "Good. I am ready."

He began with the expression of a man taking a plunge.

"Miss Wellington, I could say a great deal so far—so far as I am concerned, that I have no right to say, now…. But—are you going to marry Prince Koltsoff?"

She started forward and then sank back.

"You must not ask that," she said.

"I know—I understand," he said rapidly, "but—but—you mustn't marry him, you know."

"*Must n't!*"

"Miss Wellington, I know, it is none of my business. And yet—Don't you know," he added fiercely, "what a girl you are? I know. I have seen! You are radiant, Miss Wellington, in spirit as in face. Any man knowing what Koltsoff is, who could sit back and let you waste yourself on him would be a pup. Thornton, of the *Jefferson*, has his record. Write to Walker, *attaché* at St. Petersburg, or Cook at Paris, or Miller at London—they will tell you. Why, even in Newport—"

Jack paused in his headlong outburst and then continued more deliberately.

"It is not for me to indict the man. I could not help speaking because you are you. I cannot do any more than warn you. If I transgress, if I am merely a blundering fool—if you are not what I take you for—forget what I have said. Send me away when we return."

She had been listening to him, as in a daze. Now she shook her head.

"I shall not do that," she said. "Did you take employment with us to say what you have said to me?"

"No."

She hesitated a moment.

"I suppose all men of Koltsoff's sort are the same," she said musingly. "I am not quite so innocent as that. We are wont to accept our European noblemen as husbands with no question as to the wild oats, immediately behind them—or without considering too closely the wild oats that are to be strewn—afterwards. Ah, don't start; that is the way we expatriates are educated—no, not that; but these are the lessons we absorb. And so—" she was looking at Armitage with a hard face, "so the things that impressed you so terribly—I appreciate and thank you for your motives in speaking of them—do not appear so awful to me."

Jack, his clean mind in a whirl, was looking at her aghast.

"You—you—Anne Wellington! You don't mean that!"

She flung her hands from her.

"Thank you," she said. "Don't I? Oh, I hate it all!" she cried wildly, "the cross purposings of life; the constant groping—being unable to see clearly—the triumph of lower over higher things—I hate them all. Ah," she turned to Jack pitifully, "promise me for life, in this place of peace, the rest and purity and beauty and love of all this—promise, and I shall stay here now with you, from this minute and never leave it, though Pyramus or King Midas, as you please, beckon from beyond this mossy wall."

"Are you speaking metaphorically?" Jack's voice quivered. "For if you are, I—"

She interrupted, laughing mirthlessly.

"I do not know how I was speaking. Don't bother. I am not worth it. I might have been had I met you sooner—Jack Armitage. For I have learned of you—some things. Don't," she raised her hand as Jack bent forward to speak. "You must n't bother, really. Last night I lived with you a big, clean, thrilling experience and saw strong men doing men's work in the raw, cold, salt air—and I saw a new life. And then—" she was looking straight ahead—"then I was led into a morass where the air was heavy like the tropics, and things all strange, unreal. And why—why now the doubt which of the two I had rather believe to-night. You were too late. I bade you come to us. I am glad, I am proud that I did—for now I know the reason. But—" she smiled wanly at him, "it should have been sooner."

"Is—it—too late?" Jack's mouth was shut tight, the muscles bulging on either side of his jaw.

"Is it? You—I must wait and see. I—I dreamed last night and it was of the sea, men rushing aboard a black battleship, rising and falling on great inky waves. It was good—so good—to dream that; not the other. Wait.... It is to be lived out. I am weak.... But there is a tide in the affairs of men—and women. Perhaps you—"

She stopped abruptly.

"Let us drive out of here, Mr. Armitage. Here, in this pure, wonderful place I feel almost like Sheynstone's Jessie."

"What do you mean?" he asked sharply.

She smiled.

"Not what you thought I meant," she said gently. "Now, drive away, please."

As they returned to the house, Mr. Wellington and his friend were alighting from the touring car; Koltsoff was not with them. As soon as he saw his daughter, Mr. Wellington, whose face was flushed, called Anne to him.

"Say, Anne," he said, "is that Prince of yours a lunatic? Or what is he?

"Why, no, father. Of course not. Why do you ask?"

"Well, then, if he is n't crazy he is a plain, ordinary, damned fool. He was like a chicken with his head off all the afternoon, calling up on the telephone, sending telegrams, and then, between pauses, telling me he would have to leave right after the ball for Europe and wanting us all to sail with him. Then, at the last minute, some whiskered tramp came to the porch where we were sitting and the first thing I knew he had excused himself for the evening and was going off up the street with that hobo, both of them flapping their arms and exclaiming in each other's faces like a couple of candidates for a padded cell. Duke Ivan was a pill beside this man. And that is saying a whole lot, let me tell you."

"Why, father!" exclaimed the girl. "I could cry! We are having that dinner for him to-night, and—and oh—"

She rushed into the house and found her mother in her room.

"Mother," she said, "Prince Koltsoff has gone off again! He was with father at the Reading Room and hurried away with a man, whom father describes as a tramp, saying he must be excused for the evening."

"Very well," said Mrs. Wellington placidly; "we will have to have the play—without Hamlet, nevertheless."

"But what shall I do?"

"You might ask McCall."

"Mother! Please! What can we do?"

"Frankly, I don't know, Anne," said Mrs. Wellington. "I confess that this situation in all its ramifications has gone quite beyond me. It is altogether annoying. But let me prophesy: Koltsoff will not miss your dinner. He impresses me as a young man not altogether without brains—although they are of a sort."

Mrs. Wellington was right. Koltsoff put in an appearance in time to meet Anne's guests, but the Russian bear at the height of his moulting season—or whatever disagreeable period he undergoes—is not more impossible than was Prince Koltsoff that night.

CHAPTER XXII
THE BALL BEGINS

Mrs. Wellington's genius for organization was never better exemplified than next day, when preparations for the ball set for the night, began. At the outset it was perfectly apparent that she was not bent on breaking records—which feat, as a matter of fact, would merely have been overshadowing her best previous demonstrations of supremacy in things of this sort. There was to be no splurge. With a high European nobleman to introduce, she had no intention of having the protagonist in the evening's function overshadowed by his background. She was a student of social nuances—say rather, a master in this subtle art, and she proceeded with her plans with all the calm assurance of a field marshal with a dozen successful campaigns behind him.

Early in the day, Dawson and Buchan and Mrs. Stetson were in conference with her in her office and a bit later the servants, some thirty or forty of them, were assembled in their dining-room and assigned various duties, all of which were performed under the supervising eye of Mrs. Wellington, her daughter, or Sara Van Valkenberg. No decorative specialist, or other alien appendage to social functions on a large scale, was in attendance, and, save for the caterer's men, who arranged a hundred odd small tables on the verandas, and the electricians, who hung chandeliers at intervals above them, the arrangements were carried out by the household force.

Under the direction of Anne Wellington—whose mind seemed fully occupied with the manifold details of the duties which her mother had assigned to her—Armitage and a small group hung tapestries against the side of the house where the tables were, and then assisted the gardener and his staff in placing gladiolas about the globes of the chandeliers. Small incandescent globes of divers colors were hidden among the flowers in the gardens and an elaborate scheme of interior floral decoration was carried out. Before the afternoon was well along, all preparations had been completed and the women had gone to their rooms, where later they were served by their maids with light suppers. Armitage went to town in the car to meet the Prince, whom he had taken from The Crags at the unusually early hour of nine o'clock, and incidentally to pick up his evening clothes, which Thornton, in accordance with telephoned instructions, had left with the marine guard at the Government ferry house.

For Mrs. Wellington, whose sardonic sense of humor had not been lost in the rush of affairs, had assigned him to detective duty for the evening's function.

"McCall," she had said, "I want you to disguise yourself as a gentleman to-night and assist Chief Roberts's man in protecting the house from gentry who at times manage to gain access to the upper floors in the course of affairs of this sort. Evening dress will do—at least it is usually regarded as a good disguise, I believe."

He had received his orders, despite the sarcastic verbiage in which they were couched, with glowing emotions not easily concealed; they fitted perfectly with his preconceived determination to bring to a conclusion that night, once and for all, the situation which had brought him to The Crags.

He had, in short, resolved, come what might, to ransack Koltsoff's rooms before dawn—to dump the contents of all drawers in the middle of the floors, to cut with his knife any bags that might be locked, and in general to turn the suite inside out. For he had come to the conclusion that every one, save possibly Prince Koltsoff and the horses and dogs, knew whom he really was, and that being the case, further masquerading was nothing short of intolerable.

Then, too, yesterday's talk with Anne Wellington in Lover's Lane was running through his mind like a thread of gold, and clearly the time had come, either to meet her with identity unclouded in the minds of all, or go away and never see her again. As to the last—that depended on several things: upon second thought, upon one thing, upon Anne Wellington herself. Throughout the day in her various meetings with him, she had been markedly impersonal, tacit intimation that from now on so long as he cared to pose as an employee of the house, he must accept all the accruing conditions. He understood her position, of course, and as for his—well, he would attend to it that very night.

He found his bag waiting for him at the ferry and Prince Koltsoff at the designated place, the Reading Room. The Russian had not worked out of his irritation, not to say alarm, at the unaccountable disappearance of his chief lieutenant, but found some comfort in the fact that agents of the St. Petersburg State Department were already buzzing about Washington and Boston in regard to the matter of the Austrian mobilization plans. Armitage found him in a dogged, determined mood. He, too, was facing a situation which he meant to end that night, and his plans were all matured.

He went to his room, spent an hour or so dictating to his secretary, instructed him to call up the White Star Line in New York and book him for Friday, and then went down to the billiard room, where the men were engrossed in a close game between Marie and Willie Whipple. From here he wandered to the smoking apartment, which had begun to resemble the sample room of a wholesale liquor house. He had a servant pour him some Scotch whiskey, over which he sat for some time with thoughtful eyes, half closed. A growing uneasiness, which he could neither define nor overcome, crept over him and at length he arose and passed through the library, the morning-room, the drawing-room, even peering into the ballroom in his search for Miss Wellington. Miss Hatch was just emerging and the Prince eyed her in a peremptory way.

"Miss Wellington is not about?" he said, raising his eyebrows.

"Is not about," said Miss Hatch, who hurried away with her short, nervous steps before Koltsoff had opportunity for questioning her further.

He glared at her retreating form and was about to follow her, when Mr. Wellington interposed.

"Hello, Koltsoff," he said, "come and have a bite with us before you go upstairs. We missed you in the billiard room."

Koltsoff bowed ceremoniously.

"Thank you, but no," he replied. "I have eaten a sandwich or so in the smoking-room. If you will permit, I shall retire until the,—ah, ball."

"All right. By the way, Koltsoff, you have seemed off your feed for the past twenty-four hours. I am sorry if I upset you. You, of course, were sensible to see my position."

"Oh, perfectly," responded the Russian with an ill-concealed sneer—in fact, it was not concealed at all—as he turned toward the stairway.

When Armitage took up his position near the head of the stairs about nine-thirty o'clock, the house was ablaze with lights, but the lower floors were deserted, save for the servants loitering about the hall. These men, all in the Wellington livery—short jackets and trousers of navy blue, with old gold cord—impressed Jack, inasmuch as they suggested in some way a sense of belonging to the household, which they did naturally, and not as servants merely engaged—or loaned—for the function. Mrs. Wellington and her husband came down at ten o'clock and took a position near the ballroom door, just as a group of early arrivals trouped up the stairs. Armitage didn't approve of Mrs. Wellington. In her creamy ball gown and tiara and jewels, she was majestic and imperious to a stunning degree, but to the young naval officer—or shall we say detective—she suggested for the first time the distinction of caste. The immeasurable distance created by the millions of dollars and the social prestige of Belle Wellington and those like her, served to set them aloof from their countrymen and countrywomen. As she walked along at the side of her hulking husband she seemed the very embodiment of the aloofness of her caste. Heretofore, Jack had regarded her as a distinctly interesting, remarkably well-preserved, middle-aged gentlewoman of striking mentality, a woman whom he could like and enjoy. To-night, he admitted, she inspired in him nothing but emotions of fear.

Mentally, he fortified himself against the appearance of Anne Wellington, who, in truth, merited this precaution as she stepped past him with a slight nod and went down the stairs. She was not a bit overdone—Jack admitted that at once—and yet, how different she was from the girl in the shirtwaist suit and black hat, whom he had seen entering the sight-seeing barge the previous day, or who swathed in his navy coat, his hat pushed down over her eyes, had stood with him on the bridge of the *D'Estang*! She was all in white, slim, supple, without jewelry, save for a string of pearls about her neck. A light, filmy veil was thrown across her bare shoulders and the living curls and waves of her flawless coiffure gleamed as they caught the lights of the chandeliers. And yet—! The girlishness which Jack had found so attractive in her, was missing, and so was the characteristic animation of her features. Instead, her face was set in a formal, politely interested expression, which to Armitage seemed to change her entire personality. Yesterday she was radiant, light-hearted, impulsive, and thoroughly lovable. To-night, she was, so to say, a professional beauty, "rigged and trigged" for competition; one of a set whose ambitions, apparently, coveted no triumphs more exalted than those to be gained here, who rated artificiality as a fine art and appraised life upon the basis of standards which even the casual observer would hardly pronounce either moral or exalted.

To-night she was a professional beauty, "rigged and trigged" for competition.

To-night she was a professional beauty, "rigged and trigged" for competition.

As Armitage followed her graceful course to the side of her parents, he groaned, half humorously, and then went wandering about the upper hallway, a prey to conflicting emotions, engendered by the new point of view which the girl had unconsciously presented. A couplet of Browning's was running through his mind and more than once he found himself muttering the words:

> "Oh, the little more and how much it is,
> And the little less and what worlds away."

True! What worlds away she was to-night! Not that he had any sense of social inferiority,—he was too proud of his family for that,—but utterly alien to him and his thoughts and ideals and aspirations, she seemed. He wondered at the foolhardiness which hitherto had characterized his attitude toward her, and at the same time called himself hard names for it. Why, she was unapproachable with all her beauty and millions and methods of life! What had he been thinking of—dreaming of? His face hardened. It was not too late to cease playing the part of a fool and an ass. He would accomplish what he had come there to do and then clear out, which sensible act, he trusted, might at least serve to mitigate to some extent the opinion she must have formulated concerning him. She had had her fun, had studied and analyzed him as far as he intended she should. She might have her laugh and enjoy it to the full, but she was not to have the opportunity of laughing in his face. He went to his room, packed his bag, and then going down the rear stairway, took it out the servants' door and laid it under the hydrangeas near the main gate. When he returned, the guests were beginning to come down stairs. All his inward ease had departed. He was tense, cleared for action. All of which shows how far the emotions of an ardent nature are apt to lead a young man astray—as he was to learn before this ball was at an end.

In the meantime he followed the sights and sounds with no great interest. He was vaguely amused at the remark of a woman beyond the first bloom of youth, who, turning to her companion and nodding toward a socially famous young matron, who preceded them down the stairs fairly jingling with jewelry, remarked:

"I say, Jerry, Mrs. Billy has put on everything but the kitchen stove."

It confirmed in Jack's mind an impression which had begun to form, that the smart set, so-called, is not altogether lacking in, well,—smartness.

When the Prince entered with a ribbon and orders across his breast, the orchestra played the Russian national anthem, whereat every one arose and stood at attention. Jack noticed, however, that attention ceased and almost every one sat down during the rendering of "The Star Spangled Banner," which followed. This, he decided, might have been because no one heard it in the confusion of voices which attended the closing strains of the Russian hymn and Koltsoff's course about the room. Armitage particularly looked for Anne and located her at the Prince's side, the centre of a vivacious group. Evidently the orchestra might as well have been playing a selection from "Madame Butterfly," so far as she was concerned. This did n't help his mood and after waiting for the first dance, a quadrille in which even the elderly participated—it was given so they might—he sauntered out on the veranda and stood there gazing vacantly at the glowing *parterre* and smoking a cigarette.

CHAPTER XXIII
THE BALL CONTINUES

Groups were strolling in and out among the gardens. Armitage caught the pale flashes of fans and gowns; the cigarette lights of the men glowed among the shrubbery like fireflies. The moon was full, shining through rifted clouds, and the ocean, murmuring at the foot of the cliffs, stretched away to the starry horizon. The lamps of the Brenton's Reef light vessel seemed close enough to touch, and farther out the lights of a deep sea tug with a string of coal barges astern moved slowly down the coast.

As Jack threw away his cigarette preparatory to going into the house, Anne Wellington stepped through the door, laughing back at Koltsoff, who was following her. Jack averted his head and as he did so the girl turned to her companion.

"Pardon me for one second," she said.

"Are n't you going to ask me to dance?" she said in a low voice as she confronted Armitage.

He smiled. "Oh, certainly!"

"Oh, there is precedent," laughed Anne. "Was n't it Dick Turpin who danced with the Duchess of—of something, once?"

"But he was hanged later."

"Not for that." She stood for a moment regarding him and decided that no man at the ball was better to look at in any way. "I am a good American to-night," she said slowly. "I—I thought you might be interested to know."

"I am interested," said Jack. Then his eyes lighted. "Are you serious about that dance?"

She returned his gaze, humorously defiant.

"I don't care, if you don't," he added; "I dare you."

"They say naval officers are divine dancers," she replied as though to herself. "You may have the next dance if—if you can find me out here—and—and take me away from His Highness."

Before he could reply she had smiled and nodded and rejoined Koltsoff, who was waiting, not without impatience, at the foot of the steps. He took her arm and led the way toward a small promontory overlooking the ocean. His demeanor was silent, romantic. But somehow Anne was neither interested nor thrilled. As they stopped at the edge of the cliff, she released her arm which his fingers had tightly pressed. He took a cigarette from his case and then impatiently tossed it away.

"I spoke to your father this afternoon," he said, "as to our understanding."

"Our understanding!"

"About the dowry. He declined to yield to the European custom."

"How like father! Of course that changes your attitude toward me." Her voice was cool and unwavering.

He raised his hands as though despairing.

"It does not." He confronted her so that they almost touched. "Is it possible that you can think of that? I replied to your father that I was going to take you anyway."

"You—are going—to—take me anyway! What do you mean, Prince Koltsoff?"

"Mean! What do I mean! Why, no less than that dowry or no dowry, you are mine."

"But you have n't asked me. I have said nothing to make you believe that."

"Eh?" Koltsoff tossed his head dazedly.

"You said nothing!" he exclaimed as she remained silent. "You said—Bah! Are mere words only to serve? You lay in my arms not a day since. What words could have been so eloquent? And your eyes—the look in them! Words! Ah, Anne, could I not see? Could I not read?" His hand was on her arm but she pulled sharply back.

"Please, Prince Koltsoff! Listen! You—since you have been willing to recall it to me—did take me in your arms." Indignation was rapidly mastering her. "I did not lead you to do it. I did not want you to. I am—not that kind. I was tired, weak in mind and body and, yes,—under your control, somehow. You took advantage of it. I didn't know then—I fancied it might be love, don't you know. I even asked you if it was—"

"You asked me. I replied. You did not deny."

"No, but I deny now: It was not love."

"Not love!" Koltsoff moved close to her. "Then may I ask what it was? Surely you have not questioned *my* motives?"

- 142 -

"No. If I had, you should have known it before this. My own motives, or rather, the lack of them—but we won't talk about it any more."

She made as though to step past him but he did not move.

"But you must talk about it," he said. "Are our relations thus to be brushed away—by misunderstanding? Anne, have I been utterly misled? What is it, Anne? I command you to speak."

"Will you please let me pass?"

"No, not until you have answered me." There was crisp savagery in his voice.

Anne, now trembling with anger, turned quickly upon him.

"Very well, I shall answer you. I don't love you and I can't love you and I won't love you. I resent your actions. You have been making this house headquarters for your diplomatic schemes and when they have gone astray, you have made us all the creatures of your irritable whims. You made me a laughing stock when you backed out of the theatre party, and have done nothing but consider your own convenience irrespective of any plans I may have formed for your entertainment. You were so disagreeable last night at dinner that I wept for very shame after it. And—and—now you have your answer."

For a moment Koltsoff stood erect, as though frozen by her words. Then he bent his head forward menacingly.

Anne laughed.

"We are not in Monaco—or Russia, Prince Koltsoff, but in the United States."

"The United States!" sneered Koltsoff.

The next instant he was on his knees, his lips on the lace of her skirt.

"Please, Prince Koltsoff! Don't, please."

She glanced aside and saw the expansive white chest of Armitage bearing up the slight incline. "And now you must excuse me," she said, "my partner for the next dance claims me." She snatched away her skirt and walked rapidly to meet Jack, while Koltsoff gathered himself to his feet and cursed volubly in three languages.

Anne was silent as they walked to the house, but cheerfully so. While Jack could not exactly catch her expression in the moonlight, he had a feeling she was glad to be with him.

"Do you want to back out?" he asked. "It is n't too late, you know. Have you thought of the scandal?"

"Do you wish me to back out?" she smiled. "Have you thought you may lose your position?"

"I don't care—for you can consider that I have given notice to take effect to-morrow."

"But that does not mean—" she began, then checked herself.

He waited for her to continue, but she was silent. As they ascended the steps the orchestra was beginning the waltz, with its dreamy rhythm, which everybody had been humming for a month or two. She led the way through a door at the lower end of the room, where were the palms and shrubbery which concealed the musicians, gathered her gown in her right hand, and stood smilingly expectant. Her cheeks were deeply flushed, her eyes sparkled, her perfectly cut lips slightly parted. For an instant his eyes rested upon her face and they glowed with open admiration. Then his arm had encircled her firm, lithe waist and they whirled leisurely out upon the crowded floor.

She felt his strength, but it was the strength that exalts a woman, a strength that a woman could glory in and not feel embarrassed or self-conscious; a sense of being protected, not overwhelmed, filled her. And through the rhythm of the dance and the complete sympathy which it brought, one for the other, she caught perfectly his poise—the mental suggested through the physical—strong, determined, and so utterly masculine in a big, clean way.

The poetry of the waltz was well defined. The reputation of the Navy was losing nothing at his hands, or rather feet, as they glided in and out among the various couples, gracefully and easily. Both were exalted; it could not have been otherwise. Her supple body yielded instinctively to the guidance of his arm, seemed, indeed, almost a part of it—bodies and minds one in the interpretation of the science of rhythmic motion. Neither spoke until the floor had been circled. Then she turned her head and looked into his face.

"To-morrow?"

"Don't," said Jack, half laughing. "I don't want to think of to-morrow."

"Neither do I," she grimaced, "but I can't help it. I am going to lose my driver."

He smiled grimly, but did not reply.

"And so," she said unconsciously allowing herself to relax in his arm, "what am I going to do?" Her glance was humorously pathetic. "It has been so much fun. But it could n't last, as Trilby said."

"Some day, soon, when I have put on my uniform, may I come here and help you decide?"

"Decide what, pray?"

"You asked me what you were going to do."

She stopped dancing and looked at him with sober face.

"Well, you 'd better believe you may come here, then. You are not going to escape quite so easily. As to advice—cannot you give me that now?"

"I could," replied Jack. "But I won't—not now."

"Oh, do!" Her voice was teasing. "You can't imagine what straits I shall be in. Not that I would promise to pronounce it wise—"

They were dancing again.

"Well, then, I certainly shall hold my peace."

"Why, you 're positively bearish!"

"Am I?"

"But then, you know, I might consider your words—well, worth following."

"I 'll wait until I can find courage to take the risk."

"Is it so awfully important as all that?"

"You may judge when I tell you."

The dance had ended and as he released her she reached out and tapped him on the arm.

"You do dance divinely. And now you had better play detective. Mother has seen us."

That was quite true. Armitage, of course, had not been recognized as Miss Wellington's chauffeur by the people in the room, but Mrs. Wellington had early detected them. She said nothing until the dance ended. Then she looked at her husband.

"Ronald," she said, "is Anne too old to be spanked, do you think?"

"Why, rather, I should say. Why?" laughed Wellington.

"Oh, no matter. Only I fancy I would relinquish my hopes for eternity if I could!"

CHAPTER XXIV
THE BALL ENDS

Jack's mood would have defied analysis as he made his way through the crowded hall to the rear veranda. He peered into the smoking-room in passing and found several self-constituted Lords of Misrule holding full sway. Two young scions of great New York families were fencing with billiard cues, punctuating each other's coats with blue chalk dots and dashes, while a swaying ring cheered them on. One youth emerged from the room with steps obviously unsteady and claimed one of a pair of girls on their way to the ballroom, as his partner for the dance. She rapped him playfully with her fan.

"You don't really want a partner, Teddy," she said. "You want a hitching post. You're spifflicated."

The two moved laughingly away, leaving the young man marvelling heavily at the discernment of the girl who had cleverly discovered that which he fancied he had carefully concealed. As Armitage watched him with amused interest, he sighed deeply and made his way back to the smoking-room.

Jack went up the rear stairs to the second floor and out on a little balcony. He had viewed Miss Wellington's attitude toward him from every angle and every time the result had been the same—the conviction that her interest in him was something more than friendly. He attempted no diagnosis of his own feelings. That was not necessary; they were too patent. A great wave of tenderness thrilled him. There was wonder, too. That wonder which fills a man when he begins to realize that a girl whom he has regarded as unapproachably radiant and, in sheer beauty and purity and grace, a being aloof from most of the things of this world, finds him not unworthy of her trust, her confidence, and her love.

Armitage felt himself ennobled, set apart from the rest of mankind, the guardian of a sacred trust. If she did love him, if she were willing to give herself to him, she would find that the giving was not to be all hers. He, too, would build his life henceforth upon the inspiration she gave him and he would hold himself worthy to receive it. Anne! His arm ached to hold her as he had held her but a little while ago. Anne! The strength seemed to be going out of him. Ah, he wanted that girl now, right here—and nothing else in this world! Anne!

Then his teeth clicked shut. He had work ahead of him. There were other things to think about. In his present mood, surely, he was not up to the task he had set himself. He lighted a cigarette and puffed vigorously. If he were going to succeed—and he intended to succeed—he must train his mind rigidly into channels far remote from Anne. He must forget her; forget himself for the time being. Long he fought with himself and won, as strong men always will, and when he left the balcony there was but one thought in his mind, the magnetic control which Koltsoff had stolen from him.

He had already decided to make his search when the guests were at the tables on the veranda, and the blood pulsed quickly as he peered down the front stairs and found that all, even then, were making their way out of doors. Now—to find the Prince safely seated and engrossed, and then action. He descended the stairs and merged with the throng on the verandas. There was a great deal of confusion. Some were already seated and calling for their companions. Others were blundering about searching for friends. The complement of a few tables was already filled and there was much laughter and loud talking.

Jack soon found the Prince at a table for six, near the railing. Anne was at his side and Sara Van Valkenberg, with young Osborne, was also there. Anne was conversing brightly with a man across from her, but Koltsoff was sombre and silent. Armitage smiled and made his way into the house. He walked slowly up the stairs, went to his room, on the third floor, for a knife, skeleton keys, and a small jimmy, and then returning to the second floor he stopped at Koltsoff's door, which was well back from the apartments utilized as dressing-rooms for the men and women. The light was burning brightly in a chandelier overhead and Jack, stepping to a button in the wall, pressed it, shrouding that part of the hall in gloom.

Then he tested the knob and pushed slightly on the door. To his surprise it yielded. A thin piece of wire brushed his fingers and following it he found it led from the keyhole and outside the jamb of the door, which had been cut slightly. Evidently some one was ahead of him! But he did not hesitate. Softly opening the door he stepped into the room and closed the door behind him. Then for a moment he stood still. He felt in his pocket for his match box and had just struck a light when suddenly an arm flew around his neck from behind, the crook of the elbow pressing deeply into his throat.

Without a sound, Jack bent forward, pulling his assailant with him, despite his efforts to get Jack's head back between his shoulders. For a full minute they were poised thus. Armitage knew better than to crack his neck in frantic efforts to break the strong arm grip. There were other ways. He was very cool and he had confidence in that neck of his, which set on his shoulders like the base of a marble column. The hand of the stranger was pawing for a grip on his right wrist, but Jack, who knew the move and had no desire to have his elbow shattered, kept it out of the way. And all the time he kept up a slight strain upon the arm around his neck, into which, by the way, his chin was slightly buried, breaking in some degree the choking power of the hold.

For two minutes they stood thus, slightly swaying, and then instinctively Jack, gagging a little now, felt the minutest relaxation of the arm. Quick as thought he changed the position of his right leg, bringing into play the leverage of his hip. He twisted suddenly sideways, his neck slipping around in the encircling arm. His hand closed upon the back of a thick, perspiring neck. The next instant a figure catapulted over his back, bringing up with a bone-racking crash against a piece of furniture.

Armitage, whose eyes were now accustomed to the dark room, ran to an electric globe at the side of a writing desk and turned on the light. By this time his assailant was rising, tottering but full of fight, a desire which Jack, now all for carnage, was quite ready to satisfy. As he started for the man something in the fellow's face made him pause. He uttered a low exclamation. He was Takakika, the Japanese cook. But there was no time for words; the Jap launched himself at him with fingers quivering in anticipation of the grip he sought. He never arrived. Armitage whipped his right fist with all the power of his body behind it to a point about two inches below Takakika's left ear. There was a sharp crack and the Jap fell to the floor in a huddle, motionless.

"Now, I reckon you 'll lie still," said Jack unpityingly. "You and Koltsoff, too, will find that the spy game in the United States is full of travail."

He glanced at the man, who was groaning now and showing signs of recovery. "I guess I 'll lash you up to be on the safe side," which he did with several of Koltsoff's neckties.

"Now, then."

He arose and looked about the room. On a table near the door were several rolls of parchment. He went over to them and lifted them. They were the plans of the torpedo. With a sigh of relief he straightened them and folding the sheets into two small but bulky packages, put them into his pockets. Evidently the apartment had been thoroughly ransacked by Takakika. Drawers were opened, bags turned inside out, the bed torn apart, and the mattress ripped. But where was the control? Armitage felt about the Jap's clothing and then feverishly began going over the line of search pursued by the spy. So engrossed had he been in the struggle with Takakika that he had forgotten his intention of locking the door leading from the hall. Now his unsuccessful search filled his mind. At last in a dark corner of a closet he unearthed a small square bag. He had just taken it into the room and cut it when the door opened and Koltsoff entered.

For an instant he stood blinking and then his eyes travelled swiftly about the room, taking in Armitage, the bound and half conscious Japanese, and the general litter. Jack watched him closely, ready for any move he might make. The Russian's sudden appearance had startled him, but the first substantial thought that shot through his mind was that no one could possibly have been more welcome. He had failed to find the control: he had to have it. So he might as well have it out with the Prince now as any other time. If Koltsoff but knew it, he was facing a desperate man; for until he had entered and searched the rooms, Jack had harbored no doubt that possession of the control was merely a matter of overhauling the Prince's effects. Now he knew better, and for the first time he was really alarmed as to its whereabouts. He returned Koltsoff's gaze with smouldering eyes. But the Russian was very much at ease.

"What is it?" he asked at length. Without waiting for Armitage to reply he walked swiftly to the desk, jerked open a panel, and placed his hand in the opening. When he withdrew it, it was empty. Jack laughed, drew from his pocket a short heavy revolver with a pearl, gold-crested handle, twirled it about by the guard, and then put it back in his pocket.

"I got there first, Koltsoff," he said.

Prince Koltsoff straightened and regarded Armitage warily.

"What does this mean?" He nodded his head toward Takakika and started forward as for the first time he noticed that the man was a Japanese.

"Ah," he said, "I see. You have foiled a spy. Ha! ha! I thank you. And now the pistol—and your manner! Ha! ha! ha! Your joke!"

Armitage saw clearly that for some reason—which he believed he recognized—Koltsoff was willing that the incident, so far as Jack was concerned, should end right there. The Prince had given him his lead. He had but to follow it and clear out, with no questions asked. But that was farthest from his mind.

"My joke is not clear to you, I see."

"Indeed! Will you do me the honor to make it clear?"

"Certainly. Last Sunday night a tool of yours named Yeasky stole a magnetic contrivance from the shops of the Torpedo Station. He gave it to you. I want it. I am going to get it before either you or I leave this room."

Koltsoff clasped his hands together.

"I recognize you as a servant in the employ of this house. What right have you to address me? Now, go to your quarters at once or I shall report you. You are intoxicated!"

"Am I!" He backed before the door as Koltsoff's eyes moved toward it, covering at the same time the call buttons in the wall at the side of the jamb.

The Prince laughed and leaned carelessly back against a table.

"Very well, since you appear to deny your identity, as well as your condition—which is quite obvious, I beg you to know—I can admit only that you have the advantage of me."

"Oh, shut up!" said Jack angrily. "Are you going to give me that control? My name is Armitage. I invented that device and you and your dirty band of square-heads stole it. I want it back now, quick! And if—"

The Prince still smiling, interrupted.

"Ah, Armitage, I might have known. Allow me to say that you wore the Wellington livery with better grace than the gentleman's clothing that now adorns you—with better grace, I might even venture, than the uniform you occasionally wear."

Armitage, who quickly saw the advantage of Koltsoff's poise, curbed his anger, at least so far as speech was concerned.

"Look here, Koltsoff," he said, "let us understand each other. I am going to get that control or one or the other of us is going to be carried out of this room."

"You have the revolver—it will probably be I," said Koltsoff.

With an exclamation Jack reached into his pocket, drew out the revolver, and hurled it through the open window. They could hear it clatter on the cliffs below and then splash into the ocean. Instinctively, Koltsoff's eyes had followed the flight of the weapon. When he turned his head Jack was close at his side. The Russian stepped back. Jack moved forward.

"Now," he said in a low tense voice, "that magnetic control—quick!" There was no mistaking the quiet ferocity of his manner.

Koltsoff had ceased to smile.

"I have n't it."

"Are—you—going—to—give—me—that—control?"

"I have n't it. I swear. Look—look anywhere, everywhere. See if I do not speak the truth."

"Then get it."

Koltsoff moved to a bureau and Jack followed him.

"Wait," said the Russian. Then like lightning his hand shot out to a heavy brass candlestick and the next instant had aimed a murderous blow at Jack's head. Armitage caught the flash of the descending weapon in time to duck his head, taking the force upon the lower muscles of his neck. The wave of pain was as the lash to a mettlesome horse. Before the Prince could swing the candlestick again Armitage had him by the throat and bore him to the floor, half stifling his shriek for help.

As Armitage seized the candlestick and tossed it to one side, the knob of the door turned and the door itself partly opened. He sprang to his feet, pulled Koltsoff to his knees, and as he stood thus the door was pushed wide and Anne Wellington stepped across the threshold.

Her face was pale, her eyes were blazing.

One hand, holding a heavy package, she held behind her back. With the other she pointed to Prince Koltsoff with the imperiousness of a queen.

"What does this mean?" she asked sternly.

Behind her in the doorway the tragic face of Sara Van Valkenberg was framed.

"This—this scoundrel was trying to murder me."

Armitage was looking at her over his shoulder.

"Please don't stay here, Miss Wellington. This man stole a very important part of a torpedo that I invented. I am going to make him return it before he leaves this room."

"He says what is untrue," said Koltsoff. "It is not his property. And at all events, as I have told him, I do not possess it."

The color had returned to Anne's face. She swayed slightly as a great wave of light, of knowledge, passed over her mind.

"Oh!" Her lips moved as mechanically as those of an automaton and her face was as expressionless. "Oh!" Her eyes seemed burning through Armitage. "And you made me believe—I mean I thought—I—I—"

She bowed her head, trying to stifle tears of shame and indignation.

"Don't, Miss Wellington. Don't misunderstand! Wait until I can explain—then you will know. In the meantime I must have that torpedo, that part of it which this Russian spy stole."

"It is not yours. It is mine. And I again inform you, I have n't it."

Prince Koltsoff's sneering smile had returned.

"Wait!" cried Anne, breaking in upon Jack's angry exclamation. She stepped into the middle of the room. "Prince Koltsoff is right. He has n't it. I have it." Slowly she drew her hand from behind her back.

"Here it is."

Koltsoff stepped forward.

"It is mine!" he said. "I gave it in trust to you. I command you to keep it until I ask for it."

"He is lying, Miss Wellington. It is mine. I can prove it."

"Lying!" exclaimed Anne tragically. "Lying! Every one has lied. Where is there truth in either of you? Where is there chivalry in you and you—" nodding at Armitage and Koltsoff—"who have ruthlessly used a household and a woman to your own ends? Ugh, I detest, I hate you both! As for this," she struck the package with her hand, "I brought it here to give you, Prince Koltsoff. I could n't keep it longer. But now I think I can end your dispute for all time." Quickly she stepped to the open window and raising the bundle high, hurled it out of the window and over the cliffs.

With a dry howl of rage, Koltsoff flung himself into a chair, tearing wildly at his hair and beard, while Armitage, his hands thrust deep into his trousers pockets, stared at Anne. So far as the control was concerned, while its loss would set his work back several weeks, it at least was out of Koltsoff's hands and that naturally was the main thing. It would, in fact, have been a source of deepest joy to him had not the shock of Anne's wholly unlooked-for attitude and subsequent wild act almost unnerved him.

"A traitor! Anne Wellington a traitor!" he said in a quivering voice.

"Traitor!" Anne's voice rose almost to a wail. She turned suddenly to Koltsoff. "Of course you understand that you must leave us as soon as possible." Koltsoff, who had arisen, eyed her sullenly. She turned to Jack, who met her eyes straight. "And—and you—"

She paused and studied his face. "You—" She swayed and pressed her hand to her forehead. There was a flash of white and Sara Van Valkenberg's arms were about her. And there with her head on Sara's shoulders, she wept bitterly. The older woman caught Armitage with her eyes as she passed out of the room.

"You fool!" she said, then she bent toward him, whispering, "but don't you dare go away!"

CHAPTER XXV
THE EXPATRIATE

In the doorway Armitage paused and as Sara and Anne brushed silently past him, he turned back into the room. Without looking at Koltsoff, who was fumbling at push buttons and roaring for his valet, he walked over to Takakika, took a knife from his pocket, reached down and cut his silken fetters.

"There," he said with a grim smile, "I did n't leave you bound to the mercies of His Highness over there. Put that to my credit when you pray to the ancient Samurai."

The Jap scrambled to his feet, rolled his eyes angrily at Armitage, and then shot out of the room like a bolt from a gun. Jack followed him, making his way to the rear stairway and thus out into the night. Doggedly he strode to the clump of bushes where he had hidden the bag and his fingers were on the handle, when, with a quick exclamation, he released his hold and sat down on the turf, his head in his hands.

So this was to be the end! How quickly his house of cards had fallen! How completely had the fabric of a wonderful dream vanished to nothing! It was all coming over him strongly now for the first time as he reacted from the absorbing incidents of the past hour! Fool! Sara Van Valkenberg had characterized him unerringly. He was all of that and worse. And yet—she had done her part to make him one. He could understand exactly how Anne Wellington must have felt in view of Sara's representations to her, concerning his presence in the house, and certainly his own asinine attitude could have led the girl to believe nothing save that he had made his acceptance of employment at The Crags the excuse for a romantic desire to be near her. Yet he had not designedly deceived her. He had, of course, desired to be near her; as to that he would have been willing to attempt expedients tenfold more daring than serving as her chauffeur. That the main object of his sojourn there did not concern her was not his fault. And he had not concealed that object from her with any idea of enlisting her interest under false pretences. Ah, how he should like to tell her that now—and make her believe it!

But that opportunity had vanished, if indeed it had ever existed, during those trying moments in Koltsoff's room. In any event there was no opportunity now. Well? Once more his hand sought his bag. He might as well clear out forthwith and have an end of it all. But no; he could not, somehow. Sara's warning flashed through his mind. "Don't you dare go away!" What had she meant? Was there really some hope, which she had divined where he saw nothing but blankness? It was but a faint spark of hope but it kindled an irresistible desire to see Anne Wellington again—not to speak to her, but to fix his eyes upon her face and burn every detail of her features into his mind. He fought against it. He picked up his bag and walked toward the gate. But it was like trying to dam a flood.

As in a daze he tossed the bag back among the hydrangeas and a few minutes later found himself in the house once more, moving slowly through the crowded halls. A few of the guests were departing. At one end his questing eyes found Anne. She was shaking hands with an elderly couple and talking over her shoulder to a group of men. She was smiling but her face was feverish. For several minutes Armitage stood watching her and then resolutely facing about, he went out of doors intent upon quitting the place for good and all. As he passed around the side of the house he looked up instinctively and found himself under Koltsoff's window. Once he saw the Russian's shadow pass the illuminated square. A thought occurred to him and then somehow flashed out of his mind. It left him looking blankly up at that window, vaguely trying to traverse the mental processes which had led to the missing thought.

Then it came to him. Quickly he stepped from the path to the edge of the cliffs, perhaps twenty feet from the side of the house and guarded by a low iron railing. The moon, now, was well down in the western sky and a level path flowed across the waters to the base of the crags. He looked over the railing and a glittering object caught his eye. The revolver, in all probability. Undoubtedly the ebbing tide had left it dry. And if the weapon, thrown from Koltsoff's window, was within reach, why not the control? Armitage's face burned. It must be somewhere down there. If he could find it, much loss of time would be prevented. But more—if it *could* be found, he and not Koltsoff must be the one to recover it.

At his feet the cliffs were precipitous. He searched for the steps which he remembered were cut in the rock somewhere in the vicinity. But it was too dark; he could not find them. He must wait until the first light of dawn showed him his ground. It would save him, perhaps, a broken neck and of course simplify his search. He sat down on the grass to wait, lighting a cigar which he had taken from the smoking-room. Dancing had resumed. The measured cadence of the music flowed from the windows, and lulled by it, fatigued with all the excitement of the evening, his cigar waned and died, his head fell on the turf. He slept. He dreamed that he was dancing with Anne and that Koltsoff, with Sara Van Valkenberg as a partner, persisted in stepping upon his toes. Even in that ballroom with Mrs. Wellington's Gorgon eyes upon him the situation was getting unbearable. He hated making a scene, nevertheless—He woke with a start. The sound of wheels grinding through the gravel of the driveway brought him to his feet. It was a strange sound, eerie, uncanny. The darkness had gone, and the moon. The world was all gray; objects showed dim and ghostly; the ocean was shrouded in mist, and the wind from the face of it was clammy, heavy with salt. Moisture was dripping from the leaves, the trees, and shrubbery. The sound of laughter came from somewhere. For a moment Armitage stood irresolute, knowing that his heart was heavy and that the new day would bring no light for him.

Spiritlessly he walked to the brink of the cliffs and saw the steps upon the far side of the curve. Thither he slowly made his way. Spirals of mist were arising from below as from a caldron—old Newporters, in truth, had always known of it as the Devil's Caldron—hiding the wet, slippery fangs over or among which the swish of waters was unceasing.

As he reached the bottom he paused for an instant and then as his eyes became accustomed to the pallid gloom, he looked across an intervening stretch of about three feet of water and saw a glow of something lighter than the murk. The package! Quick as thought he stepped over to the rock and then almost stumbled over a figure in a white ball gown lying, as seemed at first impression, prone. A sickening horror passed through Jack as he bent down. It was Anne Wellington.

She lay half on her side, resting on her elbow, her skirts twining bedraggled about her ankles. With one hand she was mechanically lifting water to an ugly bruise upon her forehead. As Jack appeared at her side she smiled at him dazedly.

"There," she said, lifting her hand feebly and pointing toward a water-soaked package at her side. "I—I wanted to show you I was not a—traitor." She closed her eyes wearily. "I'm not, really, you know." As she opened her eyes, smiling wanly, Jack with a hurt cry threw himself at her side, took her in his arms, her head resting against his shoulder.

"Anne!"

"I could n't let you think—that," she said. "It would have been all right. I bungled horribly with my feet and slipped and fell." Tears were starting from Jack's eyes and she saw them. "No! No! I'm all right," she said, "just a bit dizzy. I am sorry. I was going—to—bring—it back to you—so nicely and prove I was not an expatriate." She shivered slightly and Jack drew her close.

"Don't!" he said.

For a while she lay silent while the dawn whitened and gleams of steel flashed over the waters. She was smiling now, contentedly.

"I looked all about for you after that—that dreadful scene. I couldn't find you anywhere. I was afraid—" she paused.

As Jack did not reply she looked suddenly up into his face.

"Then you can't forgive me?"

"Forgive you!"

"Sara told me all," she said. "She showed me how utterly outrageous I had been."

"Sara!" Jack inwardly breathed a prayer of gratitude to that young woman.

"Yes, she told me. But it was all so exciting, so sudden. How could I have known?" She raised her head and looked at him, her eyes all smiles and all love. "Of course it was so clear after Sara explained."

And even, in his ecstasy Jack found himself formulating a stern determination to demand at the first moment from Sara just what her explanation had been. Yet at the same time he would willingly have fallen at her feet and worshipped her.

Anne was still looking at him. Then slowly she released herself from his arms and arose to her feet. She was blushing.

"Haven't you anything to say to me—Jack?"

And now Jack blushed.

"Anything to say?" But he smiled guiltily.

"Really!" she exclaimed, frowning.

Jack came very close to her, his hands at his side, but looking straight into her eyes.

"Yes, I have something to say. I have n't any right to, but I 'm going to, just the same. Anne Wellington, I love you! I honor you! Since that night at the Grand Central Station—hang it, Anne, I can't make a speech, much as I should like to. I love you, that's all, and—and—and—" He stopped short.

She laughed that quick, fluttering laugh of happiness, much more eloquent than words. "Jack," she said, "that night I stood with you on the bridge of the *D'Estang*—then I knew I loved you."

The next instant she was crushed in his arms.

"Oh—Jack!"

There were no more words. But why words? As the tide ebbed and murmured and the birds sang in the trees above, they stood silent, immured from all the world, these two, but neither doubting nor fearing.

CHAPTER XXVI
CONCLUSION

In the library of The Crags, the light of dawn stole in through the windows and turned the brilliant light of the lamps into a pale glow. The odor of stale flowers was all about. Mrs. Wellington, with a headache, stood in the doorway. Her husband sat in an armchair with legs outstretched, smoking about his fortieth cigar. Sara Van Valkenberg stood in the middle of the floor. She had been speaking at great length and with many gestures and not once had she been interrupted. When at last she concluded, there was a long silence.

"Well, Belle?" said Ronald Wellington at last, turning his head toward his wife.

"Oh, I am not surprised," said Mrs. Wellington grimly. "I always suspected Koltsoff of some deviltry. I hoped only that it would remain beneath the surface until after the ball. It did. I have not the slightest complaint."

"So; he used this house as a rendezvous for spies!" Mr. Wellington bit at his cigar savagely. "Where is he now?"

"He motored to town an hour or two ago," replied Sara. "His secretary told Miss Hatch that they had booked for the *Metric* to-morrow."

Mr. Wellington could not repress a smile.

"Well," he said, "and where is this Armitage fellow now? Where is Anne?"

Sara laughed.

"When I last saw her she was searching for Lieutenant Armitage."

"H'mm." Mr. Wellington looked at his wife gravely. "What is it now, Belle? Have they eloped, or what?"

"I am sure I haven't the slightest idea," replied that lady yawning.

"Not interested, eh?" There was sort of a chirrup in the man's voice.

"Not the slightest," was the reply with rising emphasis. "Anne might as well marry—or elope with—Lieutenant Armitage as some one equally or more objectionable to me."

"Oh, Mrs. Wellington!" cried Sara. "Jack Armitage is eminently eligible, really. As I told you, I know all about him."

As Mrs. Wellington smiled her wintry smile and was about to reply, there was a flash of white in the doorway.

An instant later Anne had darted into the room and launched herself into her father's lap.

"Father!"

Ronald Wellington studied his daughter's flushed face for a moment, the sparkling eyes, the parted lips, the disarranged hair, the wet, bedraggled gown, and the bruised forehead.

"Where is he? Did you find him?" he asked. "You look as though you had conducted a strenuous search, Anne."

With a laugh, Anne, radiant as a spirit, ran out into the hall and when she returned she had Jack by the hand.

"Father, mother, here is Jack Armitage—Lieutenant Armitage of—of our Navy."

Mr. Wellington slowly arose.

"Say, Armitage," he said, "I know your father. He has been a mighty capable enemy of mine, or, rather, to my interests. What have you to say to that?"

Jack met his eyes with a brave smile.

"I 'm sorry to hear that, sir. But he won't be any longer. I 'll fix that."

"Of course we will," cried Anne.

"Oh!" And then Mr. Wellington's hearty laugh shook the room.

"Mother!" Anne turned to Mrs. Wellington. "Aren't you going to laugh, too?"

Something like a look of tenderness crossed the mother's face.

"I am sorry, Anne, not now." She turned to leave the room. "But I am not going to cry—be assured."

Several hours later Jack caught Sara alone.

"Sara," he said sternly, "what did you tell Anne about my being here?"

Sara smiled enigmatically.

"Really, Jack, I 've forgotten. Something to the effect that you could have sent Government detectives, had you not wanted to come here yourself."

Jack thought a moment.

"By George!" he said, "you were not far wrong!"

"Wrong!" exclaimed Sara ingenuously.

Jack stepped toward her and as he did so Anne entered the room.

"Come right in, Anne," cried Armitage, "I was just going to kiss Sara Van Valkenberg."

"Well," smiled Anne, "you may—just once."

THE END

Milton Keynes UK
Ingram Content Group UK Ltd.
UKHW030624061024
449204UK00004B/333